October 22, 1996

Eric,

Best Wish

Bottoms Up, America!

Bottoms Up, America!

Two Men, Tired of Climbing Corporate Ladders, Bicycle Across the Backroads of America in a Bold Attempt to Find a Lost Soul.

Bill Fitzpatrick
Dave Fooshe

Bellingham & Bern Publishing

Bellingham & Bern Publishing
129 Linkside Drive, Suite 202
Taylors, SC 29687

10 9 8 7 6 5 4 3 2 1

ISBN: 1-888605-22-7

Library of Congress Catalog Card No.: 95-83667

I Hear America Singing

I hear America singing, the various carols I hear,

Those of mechanics, each one singing his as it should be blithe, and strong,

The carpenter singing his as he measures his plank or beam,

The mason singing his as he makes ready for work, or leaves off work,

The boatman singing what belongs to him in his boat, the deckhand singing on the steamboat deck,

The shoemaker singing as he sits on his bench, the hatter singing as he stands,

The wood-cutter's song, the ploughboy's on his way in the morning, or at noon intermission or at sundown,

The delicious singing of the mother, or of the young wife at work, or of the girl sewing or washing,

Each singing what belongs to him or her and to none else,

The day what belongs to the day-at night the party of young fellows, robust, friendly,

Singing with open mouths their strong melodious songs.

—Walt Whitman

CONTENTS

CONTENTS

Introduction

Dave Fooshe, Ricky Borry and I are to start our dream trip in Bellingham, Washington, on May 23rd. Our goal is to pedal across the United States in around six weeks, ending up in New Bern, North Carolina—where my parents live—on or about the 4th of July. It is an aggressive schedule, one we are not sure we can make. For one thing, none of us have ever done anything like this before. I have not ridden a bike in eight years; Ricky has just purchased a new racing bike; and Dave, though a regular and consistent cyclist, has never attempted anything like this. Why? The sheer challenge of such an immense journey is one reason. It will easily be the most physically demanding adventure we have ever undertaken. It will also be a different sort of vacation. Not like snow skiing—something Dave and I have done every winter since graduating from college together—or a trip to the beach. No, this will not be your traditional, take it easy, kind of vacation.

We are also excited about the opportunity to experience our country first hand. Away from the likes of *Time* magazine, CNN, and Dan Rather. The six o'clock news always paints a much bleaker picture of this country than I, personally, have had any reason to believe. I want to find the truth—first hand.

But there is another reason, too. A more subtle, yet important reason for going. I want to search for my lost soul.

I'm not really sure when I lost it. I think I had just turned thirty—that age when you begin to feel funny dating a girl fresh out of college. Careers and climbing the corporate ladder take over. You become a target for life insurance salesmen, and you can no longer refer them to your dad. Life becomes a little more serious, and, in my view, we begin to lose our soul. I have become a single–minded, cold–hearted, white collar professional, no longer capable of smelling the roses.

I want to try and regain my soul—before it is too late.

In preparation, we pored over the map of the United States, finally selecting a scenic route that takes us through a variety of small towns and villages. What are the people like in Marblemount, Washington; we wondered, knowing we will pass through the mountain village early in our journey. Will they be the same kind of folks we'd meet in, say, Sterling, Illinois, or Prestonberg, Kentucky? Will these places we visit have their fair share of rapists, murderers and child molesters? Will we become a statistic of the highway department in some small rural town in backwoods America? Again, the news media, in its dutiful, though relentless reporting of fatalities, leads one to believe the highways are unsafe at any speed.

This perception of danger, while almost titillating to us—after all, one of the reasons we are taking this trip is to leave our safe, comfortable, and more or less predictable moorings behind for a while—gives pause to some of our nearest and dearest.

My parents, for example.

"Be sure and pack a gun," my dad advised, only half–jokingly, "there are crazy people out there."

"He's right," my mother echoed. "You're a grown man with a wife and a two–year–old daughter, should you really be leaving them all alone?"

My wife, Leith, thankfully, is more supportive. From the beginning, she was 100% behind the idea of this trip. "Bill, this is something you will always remember. You, Dave and Ricky should go ahead and enjoy this trip. Besides, I'd rather you do this than something really crazy."

This got me thinking. Why am I bent on riding a bicycle across America? Is it really to see the country and get away for a while, or am I having my mid–life crisis ten years early? Thirty–six is much too young for such foolishness.

My little girl Molly? I can only hope she will understand, and forgive her daddy for being gone so long.

—Bill Fitzpatrick, Greenville, S.C.

Part One

Getting Ready

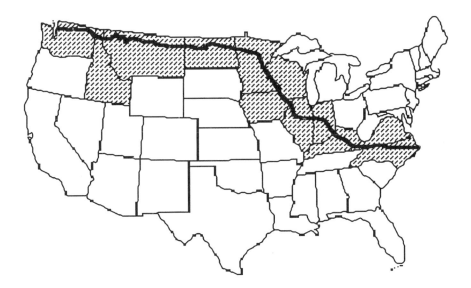

Last Rites

"For which one of you, when he wants to build a tower, does not first sit down and calculate the cost, to see if he has enough to complete it?"

—Luke 14:28

"Bless me father, for I have sinned. It has been three decades since my last confession. I just want to let you know that I have lied again."

"Again, my son?"

I sagged. Did he recognize my voice? "Yes Father, again. I stole a vacation day from AT&T. Ma Bell is a fine company, and I really work hard for them, but I still don't feel good about what I've done."

As an afterthought, I added, "But I have made my sales quota for the year." Maybe this would help reduce my sentence.

"Stealing is stealing, my son." This priest was relentless. "Are you sorry for your sin?"

I sighed. This wasn't working out at all. "No Father, I'd steal it again if I had to." No sense lying to a priest.

"Complimentary champagne?" offered the priest. I was startled. When did the church start this practice? I knew the Protestants were making gains, but this was going too far.

The question was repeated. Only it was a stewardess asking the question, not the priest.

"No ma'am. I'll take some coffee, though."

I needed coffee, too. We were on the last leg of our cross country flight from Greenville, South Carolina to Bellingham, Washington, on a day that started at 5:00 a.m. Our arrival in this small coastal town would be the beginning of our attempt to bicycle across the country to the coast of North Carolina.

For a moment, I had dozed off. Even sleep offered no respite for my jumbled nerves. Crazy Thoughts, all dressed in smart, tight fitting bike gear, pummeled my brain with their chatter. The leader of the club

5

appeared to be Why Are You Doing This. He was an impudent one, the kind of Thought that just can't leave Well Enough alone.

His most annoying trick was awakening the twin terrors, Mid–Life Crisis and Responsibility from their slumber. While Responsibility is a light sleeper, and has often troubled me over the years, Why Are You Doing This had no business stirring Mid–Life Crisis. Mid–Life wasn't due to wake up for another ten years.

Characters from my past showed up in an attempt to restore law and order to my runaway thoughts. There were several nuns, and while they looked suspiciously familiar, I couldn't find enough features to put names with the noses. As if to keep the nuns company, a priest showed up—looking just like the priest that blessed the boat I won at the second grade bazaar. He was none too pleased that I selected the boat—the other prizes were prayer books, religious chains, and statues of saints. Perhaps I should have picked the Saint of Lost Causes. A couple of old girlfriends showed up—I tried to keep them from the priest. That wouldn't do at all. And voices from my past showed up in odd snippets of conversation. However, before I could turn and find out who whispered, "Give the Money to the Poor," or "You Could Die Out There," or perhaps "Don't Ever Quit," these people scuttled away—only their shirttails were visible as they receded from memory.

I have this nervous feeling, however, that some of these characters may have unfinished business with me. If I can stay focused on the trip, and not let my mind wander, maybe they'll get the idea that the front door is locked. The priest bothers me though. He seems like the type to slip in a side window, help himself to a late afternoon drink, and make small talk, all the while trying to peer into my restless soul and point out the things that aren't quite right.

*   *   *

I'm not quite sure when I decided I had to attempt something dramatic.

Perhaps it was a year ago. I woke up one workday, and decided to radically change my life, or at least it seemed that way to me. Instead of taking my shower first, I decided to change the order of things by eating my Cheerios, and then taking my shower. It was such an important change, I even mentioned it to my wife.

"That's wonderful," she said with a yawn.

6

It was obvious she didn't get it. I tried to explain.

"I have worked for AT&T over thirteen years. Assuming a two hundred and twenty day work year, that translates to almost three thousand days in which I've taken a shower first, and then eaten my Cheerios. Don't you understand? I'm breaking with tradition."

My poor wife was lost. I think she was getting ready to call those people with the little white jackets.

I pressed on. I had to make her understand.

"Well, if you can't understand me, listen to this." And I proceeded to sing a verse from Paul Simon's "American Tune."

> *We come on the ship they call the Mayflower,*
> *We come on the ship that sailed the moon,*
> *We come in the age's most uncertain hours and*
> *Sing an American Tune.*
> *Oh, and it's all right, it's all right,*
> *You can't be forever blessed.*
> *Still tomorrow's goin' to be another working day,*
> *And I'm trying to get some rest,*
> *That's all I'm trying, to get some rest.*

Leith reached for the phone.

"You see, I want to know why I can't be forever blessed. I'm just weary to my bones—I can't get any rest. Something is gnawing at my soul, telling me it's time to do something different. I've been too long in the wind, too long in the rain. Baby, I was born to run."

Leith put down the phone and sang me a verse from "Send in the Clowns."

*　　　　*　　　　*

The years have taken their toll. After college I went right to work for AT&T and for thirteen years I have sold one product after another. Yes, the money is good, we live in a nice house, and we have a beautiful little girl. I suspect most people would look at me and say, "He has it made." And I probably do. I should; after all, my life has been programmed that way.

My three sisters and I were all raised in an upper middle class home, where Dad made the money and Mom raised the family. Golf on Saturday, church on Sunday. Going to college was not an option—it was a requirement. In fact, we all ended up with graduate degrees. Self sufficiency was ingrained in our personalities. Not a whole lot of sympathy was extended to someone with the sniffles or a light cough.

After running with the pack for ten years, at age thirty, I fell in love and married a wonderful woman, and at age thirty–four, became father to little Molly McGowan. All should be well with the world.

But if you're like me, every now and then, you have unsettling thoughts. On dark days, I pull out my mortgage and stare at the dates. In the year 2014, we'll own the house. What fabulous news that is! Sometimes I can't even remember the month or year. Were Dave and I really in college half a lifetime ago? Have I really been married for seven years? Is Molly really two? Are my parents really in their seventies? Is my little sister thirty something?

I can't even rest when I look at my old baseball cards. Roger Maris—dead. Elston Howard—dead. Roberto Clemente—dead. I'm old enough to be a father of Playboy centerfolds. After two beers, I crave aspirin and coffee. Late night is making it through the evening news.

It's time to step off the train, take a break, and find my lost soul.

I don't know what I will find on this bike trip. Or if I can even finish what I start. But I yearn for the adventure and challenge of the open road. Perhaps I will answer a few questions about myself, learn about the other people in this country, and have a good time in the process. I need to try.

*   *   *

Last night at Steak & Ale, Leith solemnly nodded her head as I shared my jumbled thoughts. I am fortunate that she is beginning to understand my need to attempt this trip. When her friends comment, "How could you let him go?" Leith says, "How could I not let him go?"

While we both know of the potential danger, we prefer not to discuss our fears. We talk instead of the challenges I will be facing. Leith expresses concern that this trip will somehow change me and affect our marriage. I don't disregard the possibility—women often see more of these dimensions than men.

When we returned home, I read little Molly a couple of stories before putting her to bed. As I closed the door to her room, the biggest fear of the trip hit me.

What if I die out there and Molly loses a daddy?

The thought stung, causing my face to blush and my conscience to wither. What is this all about, Bill? I tossed together a quick drink of bourbon, water, and guilt, and went about packing my bags.

Leith helped me load the car and then went to bed at 1:15 a.m. It took me another hour or so to pay bills, write instructions, and handle other miscellaneous tasks. Finally, the jobs were completed. I turned off the lights, and crawled into bed.

The alarm clock sounded at 4:45 a.m. and I snuck out of the house an hour later. I doubt I slept more than two hours, and my puffy swollen face showed it. I sighed, knowing that after a day of travel my condition would worsen, and leave me with a face only my mother might recognize.

I left my loving wife, adorable daughter, large mortgage, and newly increased life insurance policy to go pick up Ricky Borry.

The Young Phenom

Slow and steady wins the race

—Aesop's Fable

I met Ricky six years ago when Leith and I were the high school youth leaders for our church in Greenville. Although Ricky was but a freshman in high school, he had qualities that even then commanded respect among his peers. Ricky is now a senior at Clemson University and is majoring in chemical engineering. Near the top of his class academically, he also maintains a healthy interest in running, swimming and bicycling. One of his more modest goals is to win the Iron Man competition.

These achievements aside, Ricky is an exceptional person. His parents are both active in church, but do far more than show up for the Sunday ritual. In addition to their three children, they also have four adopted children. This has taken immense sacrifice, as Ricky's dad is the only bread winner. This environment has spawned characteristics in Ricky such as drive, determination, and thriftiness.

A month ago, Ricky and I took our first long bike ride. Our goal was to travel, round trip, from Greenville to Clemson, a distance of about eighty miles. Ricky's friend, Steve, joined us for the ride.

It was a pleasant spring morning, and we enjoyed a promising start. For the first ten miles, I pedaled away thinking that the transcontinental trip might not be so hard after all.

"Hey Ricky, maybe we can do this trip in thirty days. I feel great."

Ricky was too far away to hear me, which was just as well considering what was about to happen.

We were cycling on a crowded four lane highway through Greenville. My wheel caught the edge of the pavement and I went down in an ugly heap, my legs barely missing the tires of the passing cars. My head bounced first on the curb and then on the sidewalk. Fortunately, I was wearing a Bell helmet or I might have suffered a serious injury. As it was, the blow was severe enough for me to suddenly recall the combination to my gym locker in high school. Shaken, I got up, looked around, and since nobody I knew saw me fall, I pretended the whole thing never happened.

Steve had never bicycled more than twenty miles in one day. By the time we got to Clemson, he was visibly lagging. "Iron Man" Borry wasn't even sweating. But I was, and my pulse was still racing from my near death experience.

After stopping for lunch, we headed back to Greenville. Five minutes after leaving Clemson, it became apparent that Steve would never make it. Ricky and I waited at the crest of a modest hill for five minutes before Steve finally appeared. He was walking his bicycle, and he looked as forlorn as a bartender who takes a wrong turn and inadvertently sets up shop at a Baptist wedding.

"Why are we taking the hilly road back to Greenville?" Steve asked. "I could make it if we could just find a flat way."

A flat way? If only life were so easy!

We finally convinced Steve to call some friends and catch a ride back to Greenville. Ha! Ha! Ha! Once again, old Bill, the wily veteran, whips another young buck. I didn't think I could keep my mouth shut.

"You go on back to your mother. When you are seasoned and experienced enough, we may let you ride with us again."

That's what I was thinking. What I really said was "Gosh, I'm sorry you're not able to finish. The hills have gotten a lot tougher. I'll be lucky if I last another mile."

Late in the afternoon, Ricky and I finished our trip with a ride around Lake Robinson and a climb up Paris Mountain. As we rode by the lake, Ricky shared his thoughts about our upcoming adventure.

"I hope I'm in shape to make this trip. I've been working out hard because I want to drop a few more pounds. I figure that the less I weigh, the easier the trip will be."

Hopes he can make it? I wonder what chance he thinks I have? He's on the swim team, works out with the bike team, runs track in his spare time, and is barely twenty–one. Unless you count Little League baseball, I never made a team. And why is he trying to lose weight?

"On a three man tour, Ricky, you are only as fast as the slowest rider. That will be me, so relax, eat up and gain some weight, because we will be burning more calories than we can consume."

He nodded, but didn't really listen. As I labored around the corner of Lake Robinson, Ricky pulled ahead of me. To be sure, my fat oversized touring tires were no match for his skinny racing tires, but we could have switched bikes and the results would have been the same. Dave and I will have a tough time keeping up with the young buck.

Sweating and swearing, I lost Ricky on the climb up Paris Mountain. I can picture him finishing the trip way ahead of us, and with extra time on his hands, take the opportunity to rest on a North Carolina beach. Occasionally, he might shift his beach chair to the west, in a half-hearted attempt to find his missing friends. He wouldn't be able to find us though. Dave and I would still be in the cornfields, dodging the cornflies, cornsnakes, and other dangerous cornthings that hide out in Iowa. At least we'll be together in our misery though, and can help each other in the event one of us is felled by a corntruck.

*   *   *

At 6:00 a.m., I rolled into the Borry's driveway. His parents were both awake and helping Ricky with last minute packing. While Ricky and his dad loaded my car, his mother, Margaret, took me aside.

"Bill, I want to remind you that Ricky is not your responsibility. He's an adult, and capable of making his own decisions. So please don't worry about him on your trip. You are not accountable for his well-being."

It was very kind of her to say that. I don't worry much about Dave—he is an experienced traveler—but I do worry about Ricky.

The time had come for us to leave. Dick and Margaret each said a prayer, and after many hugs, Ricky and I left for the airport. As we drove away, I peered back through the early morning dusk, and saw his parents, holding hands, slowly walk back to their loving Christian home.

My Old College Roommate

Man's best support is a very dear friend.

—Marcus Tullius Cicero (106–43 B.C.)

In the Seattle airport, Ricky and I caught up with Dave Fooshe, the third member of our intrepid force. He didn't look intrepid, though. He looked like he had stopped at a bar on the way home from work and had left only when his pockets were filled with bar napkins and a large assortment of coins.

"No I didn't go out drinking," Dave said in response to my query, "I had other problems. I was up until 2:00 a.m. packing my panniers."

Panniers are canvas saddlebags that fit over and around both the front and rear tires of a bike. In theory, they will hold all our material needs for the next six weeks.

"I taped the bike box closed and stepped back to congratulate myself on a remarkable job. Feeling smug, I looked up and saw that I had forgotten to pack my wheels. Two hours later, I finally got to sleep."

Dave is easily the most experienced cyclist in our group. He has put in thousands of miles on his bicycle including a recent trip down the Pacific coast. My only major bike trip was a five hundred mile tour of Quebec and Ontario, and that was eight years ago. Ricky has never been on a bike tour.

Dave and I were roommates at the University of South Carolina. Through the years, my other college friends and I have gone our separate ways, but Dave and I stay in touch, and even manage to get together once or twice a year. Dave is an engineer for an aerospace company in Redondo Beach, California.

About a month ago, I was in Los Angeles on business, and had an opportunity to visit Dave. He had recently purchased a new, lightweight, racing bike, so I borrowed his old touring bike and we went for a ride up to Malibu.

13

Our route took us along a bike path through Marina del Rey and up to Santa Monica. From there, we dropped down to the Pacific Coast Highway and headed north through the Malibu hills past Zuma Beach. I was running out of energy as we approached Neptune's Pit, a surfer hangout, noted for cheap food and buxom blondes.

"I've been riding bikes since I was six," Dave said during breakfast, "and, at the age of twelve, I went on a Boy Scout camping trip by bicycle. I guess that was my first official bike tour, although no one called it that. I really enjoyed myself. It wasn't until much later, however, when I saw the Race Across America on television, that I realized I wanted to cycle across the country."

The Race Across America is an annual event that provides a few insanely dedicated athletes the opportunity to compete for the glory of winning a coast–to–coast bike race. Contestants often pedal forty–eight hours without sleep, in an all out assault to win. While Dave, Ricky and I plan to take six weeks for our trip, the winning time for the Race Across America is usually around eight days.

"Another reason I'm looking forward to this trip is to satisfy the old travel bug. It's fun getting out and seeing other places. That's how I ended up in California. After college it was Baltimore. The next stop was Tucson, and finally Redondo Beach. The next job always seemed more exciting and interesting than the current one. After a while, though, the big cities are all alike. I'm ready to see 'small town' America, again."

But Dave, do you think that two old warriors can make it?

He laughed, "I've only known one other person who has ridden a bike across the country. Kenny Gioseffi, a cycling friend, did it solo. He talks about the hardships of the road, the friendly people, and the loneliness that you sometimes feel. But mostly, he says it was an adventure he will never forget.

"It should be easier for us, though. Together, we survived some wild times in college, and we did manage to live together for a year without major difficulties. I know we will have to depend on each other on the trip, and of all my old college buddies, I trust you the most."

That was easy for Dave to say. I am the only college buddy with whom he stays in touch.

I asked Dave the question that's been pounding in my brain the last few months, "Do you think I'm ready for this?"

"Sure you are," he replied, "Beyond getting in reasonable shape, you can't really train for this trip other than by doing it. You are certainly holding your own today. This is the route I used to train for the

Pacific coast tour I took a few years ago. If you can complete this ride, you will do just fine."

At the end of the ride, we had logged one hundred and twelve miles, which was the furthest I had ever ridden in a day. I felt surprisingly good, with none of the same defeated feelings I had after the Clemson ride with Ricky.

Maybe I am ready for this trip after all.

Part Two

No Place For The Innocent

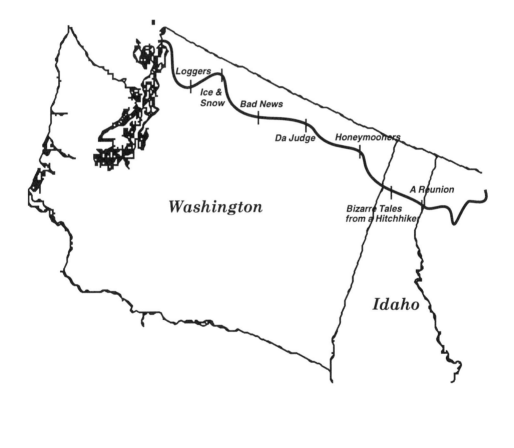

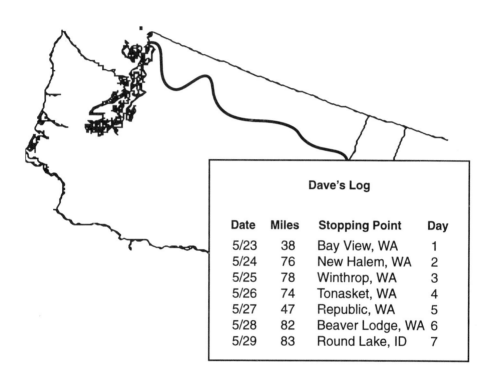

Dave's Log

Date	Miles	Stopping Point	Day
5/23	38	Bay View, WA	1
5/24	76	New Halem, WA	2
5/25	78	Winthrop, WA	3
5/26	74	Tonasket, WA	4
5/27	47	Republic, WA	5
5/28	82	Beaver Lodge, WA	6
5/29	83	Round Lake, ID	7

Scenery: ★ ★ ★ ★ ★
Fabulous. A wide variety of terrain, including snowy peaks, not–so–tropical rain forests, and semi–arid farmland.

Roads: ★ ★ ★ ★ ★
Plenty of wide shoulders, and mostly light traffic.

People: ★ ★ ★ ★ ★
I promise I won't quote Barbra "don't call me Barbara" Streisand again.
"People, who need people, are the luckiest people…"

Weather: ★
"Look at the positive side," I told Dave. "It's not like it snowed on us every day. Let's go ahead and give it a star."

The First Miles

Count the cost before you commit yourselves

—Aesop's Fable

The small Bellingham airport was perfectly suited for arriving cyclists. Outside the main terminal building was a large loading dock, which was an ideal place to unpack our gear and assemble the bikes.

In theory, we each should have needed an equal amount of floor space for our equipment. After all, we had spent months agreeing on a common packing list. As we started our work, however, I noticed that Ricky's inventory occupied a very small area. My gear took up a slightly larger space. But Dave? His stuff took at least half the available area, and that still wasn't enough. People in the airport kept looking out, as if concerned that his spread might ooze into the main terminal and take over the entire airport.

"What did you bring?" Ricky asked Dave. "I think you've got too much junk in there." The student had a good point.

"What haven't you brought?" replied Dave. The engineer had a good point. I wondered if he had decided to scratch any items from the original list.

"You guys figure it out later. I'm ready to hit it," I said, and pedaled smartly towards town.

I'm sure I looked great for about ten feet, then my front handle bars gave way—I had forgotten to tighten them. Dave and Ricky looked on in disbelief and said to each other, "We're riding across the country with this guy?"

Slightly embarrassed, I made the repair, and started again. I rode another ten feet and my left rear pannier fell off. Laughter erupted from the packing area. I started to say something clever, but decided to hold all comments until I had gone at least fifteen feet. I soon realized that I had mounted my rear panniers on the wrong sides. The right was

19

on the left and the left was on the right, and every full cycle of the pedal would knock a bag off.

After our slow start, we finally departed the small town of Bellingham and rode along the scenic Washington coastline. The cloudy and cool conditions made for a fine afternoon of cycling.

"We're on our way, we're on our way," a small voice inside me shouted. A smaller voice inside me was more pragmatic. "Don't get too high or low during the trip," it whispered.

The smallest voice had a more sinister tone. "This is your command center. We're obligated to inform you that we don't think you'll make it. We're starting a pool to pick the precise date you'll quit. Would you like a piece of the action?"

Dave and I got our first taste of discipline late in the afternoon. As we swooped around a graceful downhill curve, the spectacular beauty of the Pacific Northwest was unexpectedly enhanced by the sudden appearance of a rundown, shabby, immensely inviting oyster bar. We shouted triumphantly, and slowed to stop. Ricky slowed, more out of polite curiosity.

"What do you think Bill, should we stop?" asked Dave.

I paused and reconsidered. It took a few seconds to answer Dave, my lips had already compressed to start the "B" in Budweiser.

"Bu–uh–let's move on Dave," I said. My lips had a mind of their own and were slow to react. "I guess if we stop at every tempting oyster bar, we'll never make it out of this state. On the other hand, we could write a best–selling book titled *The Great Rundown Oyster Bars of Washington State.*" An hour or so before dusk, with the book idea forgotten, we pulled into Bay View State Park.

After setting up camp, we celebrated our first day on the road with dinner at the Farmhouse Inn, about two miles from the campground. It was fun sharing our plans with the diners and employees, but I'm not sure they believed we were about to cycle across the country. For one thing, we were jabbering like charter members of the blue-haired ladies bridge club in Hoboken, New Jersey. Our attire didn't help either. With our freshly laundered clothes, we looked more like models for a biking magazine than serious touring cyclists. After our dinner, we returned to camp and crawled into our sleeping bags.

*   *   *

Despite waking at 5:00 a.m., we didn't leave the campground until two hours later. It had rained during the night and soaked our tents and sleeping bags. As I soon learned, wet gear means extra weight. We wasted at least an hour waiting for our gear to dry.

Before leaving the campground, I made the ultimate commitment. I tossed my return plane ticket into the trash. Ricky and I had purchased round trip tickets from Greenville to Bellingham, because they were less expensive than the one–way fare.

"Uh, Bill, you may need that ticket," Ricky said. I think Ricky's confidence in my abilities was shaken by my problems back at the airport. "I'll fish it out of the dumpster if you'd like."

"Nope. Let's go. I don't want that ticket in my bag." Ricky continued to stare at me and the dumpster. "It's a psychological thing," I added weakly. "C'mon, let's fill up our water vials."

Padilla Bay represents the westernmost point of our journey. Our plan was to fill our small vials with water from each coast, as permanent reminders of our trip. We all came properly equipped for this task, and with the little vials handy, we left the campground on our bikes and began the race to the water. Each of us wanted to be the first to achieve this noble ceremonial feat. Don't ask me why grown men act this way. Please don't ask my wife, either.

After about a half mile, my buddies left me behind. As I suspected, I will be the slowest in the group. When I came around the last corner before the bay, I was shocked to see Ricky and Dave waiting patiently by their bikes. What friends! They were waiting for me so we could dip our vials in the water together.

"Thanks for waiting, guys!" I shouted. "I'm ready. Lets get on with the ceremony."

Dave broke the news.

"Low tide, Bill. I don't know about you, but I'm not going to get knee deep in the muck just for a water sample. If you go, though, I'll be glad to take your picture. I'll also let you fill up my water vial."

Without a word, I got back on my bike and led the way towards the towns of Sedro Wooley, Concrete and Marblemount.

Loggers

An environmentalist had been talking for some time about the importance of old growth forests when a puzzled congressman interrupted to ask, "Okra? What's this okra you're talking about?"

—Keith Ervin,
Fragile Majesty

"Welcome to Concrete! Should have been here a couple of months ago. We had our annual lumberjack festival. It was wild! You ever seen fellas being tossed out of bars through plate glass windows? Well, that ain't nothing. This one fella got tossed in one window, and then two minutes later, out the other! The beer cans were at least four inches deep down Main Street."

"Oh yes," I said. "That would have been fun."

We were talking with Paul, a third generation lumberjack. We had stopped for lunch in the small unassuming town of Concrete. It felt good to stretch and relax. For two hours we had labored along the historic Skagit River, anticipating a warm restaurant and a hearty lunch.

The road along the Skagit had been rough. Potholes, no doubt caused by logging trucks that haul trees out of the forest, slowed our speed along the river. The damp afternoon, combined with a cool breeze, chilled us during our occasional stops. Despite the conditions, however, it had been an enjoyable scenic ride.

On occasion, though, it was not as scenic. On both sides of the river, were ugly brown slashes of earth that were unprotected by trees, and therefore, exposed to the harsh Washington weather. The result? Thick brown goopy run–off that occasionally covered the highway, and made us feel like we were cycling in five inches of cold molasses.

Just before Concrete, we crossed over the river on our way to the town, and stopped on the bridge to admire the view. In the blink of an eye we could see Indians canoeing down the river, rowing in concert with the rhythm of the water. In another blink of the eye, we could imagine fur traders camping along the shore, examining their pelts. And today, we had seen huge logs floating in the Skagit on their way down to the sawmills.

There was not much to the town of Concrete. A few stark buildings constructed of either brick or concrete blocks were all that were there. Some had stood the test of time. Some hadn't. We leaned our bikes against the outside of a restaurant and headed inside.

Like the town, it was an unpretentious establishment. Plain yellow tablecloths covered the few wooden tables. Old framed pictures hung on the walls—many of the photographs dated back to the early part of the century.

There were a total of ten diners in the restaurant. All wore clothes right out of the 1959 Sears catalog. Their flannel shirts were all faded, and their jeans were covered with grime thick enough to scare away Mr. Clean. We seated ourselves at a large table and studied the menu. The restaurant was quiet—we were definitely the object of scrutiny. A booming voice in the corner interrupted the silence. We were about to meet our first lumberjack.

Paul, in his early forties, has cut timber most of his adult life. Despite his heritage, however, he sees the warning signs. He spoke at length about how the large paper companies have put the local people out of work by automating the tree cutting process. Today's saws cut the trees right at the ground level. He said that he is in favor of groups such as the Nature Conservancy buying land to protect it for future generations. We did not expect to hear this from a lumberjack.

"We have a bigger problem," Paul said, "All these trees being cut? Local companies don't get a penny. Most of the trees are being shipped to the Japanese, without even touching our lumber mills. Our own people are out of work and mills are going out of business because the big companies get better deals overseas. So there you have it. Our land is being stripped and on top of that, we're losing jobs. Last year, over one-third of our lumber went right to Japan without even touching the local mills."

As Paul continued to talk, I stared outside the window to the little blue collar town of Concrete. Most of the buildings at one time probably had fresh coats of paint covering the ugly concrete blocks. Now, the paint in many places was faded and splotchy—not unlike the town's apparent future. The rains have eroded much of the exterior color and freed it to flow down the Skagit River. Perhaps the paint keeps the logs company.

I've never been in a blue collar town before. I've always thought that our country is made up of lots of different people, all working and

23

playing together, but as Paul was speaking, it occurred to me that I was wrong. Blue collar workers hang out with other blue collar workers, and white collar managers pal around with other white collar managers. We all live in separate neighborhoods, every bit as segregated as the box seats and bleacher slabs in a ballpark.

Paul described in greater detail the extent of the devastation.

"The last few years, Oregon and Washington have set records for lumber production. Despite this, the number of workers required to produce the lumber continues to drop. And the weasly Forest Service ranger I was talking to the other day predicts that this number will continue to fall."

Paul is leaving the lumber business. He is heading to Alaska to "watch oysters" as he put it. He is serious—evidently the U.S. government is doing a study of the oyster and Paul has managed to land the position. I tried to absorb the spectacle; this bearded third generation lumberjack with clipboard, sitting in a chair, intently staring at an oyster bed. His girlfriend was with him in the restaurant. She, too, is planning to go to Alaska.

I wondered what his ancestors would think of all this? Their pictures lined the walls of the restaurant. Paul had proudly pointed them out.

Gradually, talk shifted to our trip. By this time, all of the restaurant patrons were listening with rapt attention as we described our intentions. After all of seventy–five miles, we fancied ourselves seasoned experts. We casually answered questions, took deep confident swallows of our drinks, and in short, behaved exactly like the neon–colored, polypropylene–covered, pink–cheeked innocents, that we were.

After lunch, as we stretched our muscles in the cool, damp air outside the restaurant, I had a few minutes to consider the small town of Concrete, Washington. Only on a bicycle would you stop in a place like this. Although the food had been very good, no self respecting Dad would haul his family into this town, and no responsible Mother would let her kids dine in this faded, ugly slab of a building.

And she certainly wouldn't let you go to the bathroom there.

Where's My Plane Ticket?

Am I again a victim of delusion? That streaming throng of spirits—gone are they? Dreamt I the Devil through some mere illusion. Or did a poodle only leap away?"

—Johann Wolfgang Von Goethe,
Faust

The fifteen miles from the restaurant did not dampen our confident spirits. We easily covered the rolling terrain, and arrived in the small town of Marblemount. It is advertised as the "Gateway to the American Alps."

The what? Was this payback for a long forgotten sin committed in my geography class? I have never heard of the American Alps.

I paced the sidewalk, alternately staring at the small rectangular sign, and then the road that led into these newly discovered mountains. Nervously, I tore at my handlebar bag, and rummaged through the assorted maps and books, looking for more information. Maybe there was an overlooked article such as "Guide to Surviving the American Alps on Bicycle," or better, "Town of Marblemount Misleads Tourists with Hype and False Advertising."

While I was pondering my fate, Dave and Ricky had been grocery shopping inside a small store. It took nearly an hour, something that didn't surprise me. I have been shopping with Dave before. But for Ricky, it was a unique experience, and he came out questioning the amount of money spent, and the large quantities of food that were purchased. Thankfully, Ricky had plenty of room in his front panniers, so we loaded him up with the four bags of groceries. After doubling the weight of Ricky's bike, we, more or less harmoniously, headed into the drizzly, foggy American Alps.

*   *   *

The light rain continued for a few miles after our departure from Marblemount. Dave and I were so confident that it wouldn't get any worse, we neglected to put on our full rain gear. Dave's Gortex jacket was safely tucked in his rear pannier, and my neoprene booties, that I had purchased to protect my only pair of shoes, remained nice and dry in my front pannier. Of course, the gods punished us for trying to predict the weather, and Dave and I were soon reduced to quivering rain-soaked fools.

Dave and Ricky, the experienced campers, had mentioned that our destination for the evening was a federal campground. They put special emphasis on the word "federal." To me, federal meant bigger and better. Perhaps there would be fluffy white towels after we took our showers. Maybe the rec room would have ping pong tables. I asked Dave for some details.

"The federal campgrounds I've used have never had hot showers. Sometimes, they didn't even have restrooms. This really peeves me considering all the taxes I have paid. What did you expect, anyway?" he asked curiously.

I didn't respond. Dave didn't know that last night was the first time I had ever camped.

Three miles from the campground, the raw cold rain dampened even Ricky's spirits. Perhaps to keep his mind off his frozen feet, he asked how my Neoprene booties were holding up. Because of his front running status, he was unaware that I had not put them on. "Oh they're doing fine," I snarled.

We arrived at the campground. Dave was right. No showers. One outhouse. Overhead, the sky was barely visible through the thick, dripping layers of trees, vines and ferns. Our campsite was surrounded by moss on every tree and rock, indicating that rainfall was a common event.

"I'll start dinner," Dave said, "as soon as I change into some dry clothes." He disappeared into his tent with a bit of a swagger, as if to emphasize the wisdom and value in overpacking.

Ricky and I exchanged pained expressions, for everything we had was cold, wet and useless. In a few minutes, Mr. Preparation reappeared in dry blue jeans, a thick corduroy shirt, dry shoes and socks, and a sporty-looking Gortex windbreaker. He went cheerfully about his job of preparing a hot dinner of pasta and Prego, even having the nerve to whistle a bit while cooking. Ricky and I huddled together, looking as miserable and pathetic as abandoned dogs. Fifteen minutes later, Dave announced dinner, and we all sat down to eat.

"What a great meal," Dave said, innocently.

I've known Dave a long time and refused to take the bait. "It's terrible," I said, "I hope your cooking improves, so we don't have to waste all our money eating in restaurants."

Ricky plunged headlong into the trap.

"I don't know what Bill is talking about. This stuff is great. It really hits the spot."

Ricky had done it. He swallowed the bait as quickly as he had swallowed the delicious food.

"Sure beats peanut butter," Dave smirked.

Ricky's pained expression returned.

My pained expression had never left my face. I was too busy worrying about some things I'd forgotten to pack.

I couldn't find my second pair of riding shorts. Had I forgotten to pack them? Would I have to wear my one pair until we came to a bike shop? I had forgotten to pack a pillow, too.

At three in the morning, I discovered that my mattress pad was too short. Heavy rains swamped the tent, and the only dry place was on the short mattress, or should I say raft? I scrunched my six–foot, two–inch frame onto the tiny four–foot pad, and found that while I could keep the end of the bag dry, I could only maintain the cramped position for about eighteen seconds because my kneecaps blocked my breathing. I put my feet back in the puddle and happily remembered that I had saved fifteen dollars on the shorter mattress. The rest of the night I tossed and turned in sleepless misery.

In the morning, three surly and grizzled cyclists gobbled up blueberry pancakes, and left, well, like bats out of hell, from the federal campground. I was in a crabby mood.

"Those pancakes were awful," I told Dave, "it will be your fault if I can't finish the climb today."

Stairway to Heaven

And I dreamed I was dying,
I dreamed that my soul rose, unexpectedly,
And looking back down at me, smiled reassuringly.
And I dreamed I was flying.

—Paul Simon,
American Tune

I was confident as we left the federal campground, that nothing could be worse than the night of misery we had just experienced. I was wrong. At Ross Dam, we turned into gusting winds, and began a brutal, forty–two mile climb towards the peaks of the Cascade Mountains.

My eyes strained to find a warm restaurant, or a heated rest stop. Many roadways in the south have such places—they offer big maps of the state, and a few suggestions on where to spend money. After an hour, I gave up. It was apparent that environmentalists had designed the Cascade Highway with only ozone eating cars in mind— how else to explain the complete lack of services for so many miles?

To be fair, it is important to note that there were a number of uncleaned, unheated, rest areas available for the occasional cyclist suffering from hypothermia. I had read about hypothermia before the trip:

hypothermia (hi–po–therm–e–a)

noun

1. a condition caused by a quick drop in the body's inner–core temperature resulting in uncontrollable shivering and can lead to sudden death.

related topics (see novice cyclists)

Close to noon, in an effort to stay dry from the rain, we pulled into one of these spartan outposts. Ricky, who was riding ahead of us, was already there, and wanted us to go exploring.

Dave wearily said, "You go ahead, Ricky, Bill and I need to rest." Dave and I were both exhausted and in no mood for frivolous adventure.

Once again my body shook with cold. Was I shaking because I was hungry and needed food? No, I had already eaten three peanut butter sandwiches and several food bars, but the shakes continued. Dave and I huddled beneath the overhang of the roof, but were still not protected from the rain. We could have gotten out of the rain if we had gone into the outhouse, but we decided rain was the better alternative.

Dave barely said a word during lunch, most of the time he was content to stretch his muscles, and mutter an occasional "damn." Often he stared into the distance, as if he was attempting to quell inner voices. More than once he said, "my back hurts," in his quiet, unassuming way.

Our young friend returned. "It was neat! You guys should come with me and see the waterfalls—they are only a mile or so away."

"Not this time, Ricky," I said. "Let's get moving." I got back on my bike, and coaxed exhausted leg muscles into continuing the climb.

Barely a mile from the rest area, Dave and Ricky pulled away from me, and I was left to pedal alone. I didn't really mind, for there was minimal traffic, and the shoulders were wide enough to accommodate my uneven cycling. Every thirty minutes they slowed down and waited to make sure that I was OK. We did manage one group break.

"I'm worried about you Bill," Ricky said. "Your face is pale, and you're sweating far too much. You feel okay?"

"I'll make it," I responded sarcastically. How should I feel after-sleepless nights, time zone changes, lousy food and pure fatigue?

Dave didn't say a word during the stop. He again stretched his back, and stared at the highway that curled into the clouds. When we took off, Dave dropped behind me, and even further behind Ricky.

Bong! Bong! Bong! Sleet and snow pelted my hard shell helmet. The head protection saved me from any physical damage, but there was nothing to protect my inner spirit. For some peculiar reason, I kept mumbling the same refrain from "American Pie."

> *"And in the streets the children screamed,*
> *the lovers cried and the poets dreamed,*
> *But not a word was spoken,*
> *the church bells all were broken.*
> *And the three men I admire most,*
> *the Father, Son, and the Holy Ghost,*
> *They caught the last train for the coast*
> *the day, the music died."*

Don't ask me why.

Thighs burned like bare feet on a hot sidewalk. Neck muscles were locked in a torturous position, either from fear, cold, or fatigue. During breaks, I slowly twisted my neck, hoping to restore movement, and also hoping that a muscle wouldn't snap in the chilling wind. How much further was there to go?

There were no mileage signs that said, for example, "Rainy Pass 18 miles," or "Washington Pass 22 miles." Our private hells were measured not in miles remaining, but in degrees of pain, and thresholds of mental anguish. The long, lonely, icy road stretched ahead of us, its limits only defined by the boundaries of our imaginations.

Every thirty minutes I stopped and waited for my old buddy. I'd peer down the hill, intent on finding a red–clad cyclist through the swirling snow and hellish ice bullets. Dave's arrival took progressively longer—the first break I waited five minutes, the second, ten minutes. And now, the last break before Rainy Pass, a full fifteen minutes had passed. Finally, Dave appeared. His unsteady form crested a small hill, and ever so slowly, closed the distance between us. On his arrival, it was apparent from his expression that something had happened.

"I don't know how to tell you this," he said. "I just had an incredible experience."

I nodded encouragement.

"I have never been in such excruciating agony. Sharp pains shot through my back, and I began to question myself. What am I doing out here? Who am I trying to impress? Never have I been in such agony."

Dave wasn't through. He stared at me intently, as if to say, "Old roommate, we've known each other a long time and have told a lot of tales, but what I am about to tell you is the truth."

"Perhaps the mental anguish was too much, and I could no longer deal with reality. Who knows? Anyway, the last bolt of pain shot up my spine, and exploded in my brain. Suddenly, the pain stopped. A peaceful, serene feeling enveloped all of my senses. I remember coming out of my body, and staring down at my poor, struggling self. I then unloaded on myself.

"'Self, you wanted to take this trip, it was your idea to ride a bicycle across the country, so quit your whining and complaining, and get on with it!.' Amazingly, after that, the pain lifted. I felt as though I were floating on a cloud.

"I have read accounts of people having out–of–body experiences, never dreaming that it might happen to me. Then again, I have never been in such pain. I have heard that when you die, something similar happens. In fact, I once saw a movie in which the ghost of a person arose from his body as he drew his final breath. Although it was only a movie, an odd feeling come over me. A few years later, I saw the movie again. Remembering the scene, I prepared myself for what was to come, but I still felt the same sensation. Perhaps experiences such as these prepare us for death?"

Awkward silence followed Dave's story—I simply didn't know what else to say. This was deep. I finally managed, "C'mon, Dave, let's finish the climb."

*   *   *

We were an exhausted lot at the top of Washington Pass. Even Ricky looked a bit awed by the experience. A few pictures were taken, but we didn't stay long—once again I began to shiver as if I'd gone for a naked dip in the North Atlantic. Concerned about hypothermia, we quickly ended our celebration and began the descent.

What should have been an enjoyable downhill ride turned into a grueling challenge. Every muscle strained to wring the last bit of heat out of my system. I couldn't trust my frozen hands to react at high speeds, so I kept below ten m.p.h. by braking all the way down the mountain.

The air gradually warmed on the descent towards the town of Mazama. By the time I caught up with Dave and Ricky, the shakes had stopped. I stripped off my damp layers, and exposed my skin to the warmth of the sun. The climate was markedly different, it was warmer and drier. I had survived.

We could have stayed in Mazama, but we felt so good we pedaled the fifteen miles to Winthrop. This, too, was not without challenge. The highway was under construction, so we had to walk our bikes for at least three miles. I didn't complain. It was beautiful countryside, and it was a nice warm, late spring afternoon.

*   *   *

The one hundred miles between Concrete and Winthrop were hellish. Every possible test was thrown our way—cold rain, sleet, snow, an endless uphill climb, and one out–of–body experience. The only thing Dave or I wanted to do was find a motel room with a comfortable bed and hot showers. Ricky had other ideas.

"I don't want to stay in a motel room," he said, "I prefer to camp out. After all, I thought this bike trip was supposed to be an outdoor experience."

"But Ricky, Dave and I have already had an outdoor experience today. Don't worry about the money. We'll pick up the cost of the room."

"No, I really want to camp. Even when I used to go on vacation with my family, I preferred to sleep on the floor in my sleeping bag. You guys go ahead and check into a motel and I'll find a campground."

Unfortunately, because this is Memorial Day weekend, the Polo shirt and Chardonnay crowd had booked every last room in the city. Winthrop is a tourist town, and a favorite destination of yuppies from Seattle. Dave and I caught up with Ricky, and told him we would be camping with him, after all. First, though, we all agreed to get a bite to eat.

On first appearance, the town is attractive and inviting. False storefronts are the rule—the facades neatly cover the old brick and blocks of another era. Prosperous people saunter down the sidewalk, every now and then glancing over their shoulders to check on the well–being of their BMW's.

"I've never really liked people who own BMW's," I said to Ricky and Dave. "They are too snobbish for me. It's as if they are saying, 'Hey, look at me. I got lots of money.' Same thing with this town. It's also pre–occupied with looks and images."

I was warming to the topic when I remembered that my sister, Bonnie, drives a BMW, and I like her a lot.

"You'd never find a BMW in Concrete," I added lamely, and hoisted my beer glass as if I'd made a very important point.

Dave didn't acknowledge my last comment. He had this dreamy look in his eyes, as though he were still back there on Rainy Pass, floating along the highway.

Our feast in Winthrop completed, we sucked down the dregs of our last beer, wove our way through hanging ferns, and rode back to the campground.

A Twist In The Road

Experience is a good school,
but the fees are high.

—Heinrich Heine

In preparation for the trip, Dave and I read a lot about "what to pack" for a major bicycle tour. We freely took the advice of others, and compiled an inventory of all suggested items. I remember sharing this list with Ricky. Sometimes he nodded in agreement, but mostly he told me that he didn't need the suggested item. We had an animated discussion on the value of bicycling tights two days before we left home.

"You've got to buy some protection for your legs, Ricky. Every book I've read says that in temperatures below sixty degrees, tights should be worn. It will get below that, so buy some. I've read accounts of people suffering from hypothermia, even in the summer, so why take the risk?"

"I won't need them," he said. "I've been riding around in temperatures below sixty degrees, and haven't had any problems."

"If you don't want to spend the money on tights," I countered, "at least get some stockings." Was money the issue? Dave and I have worked for years, so we don't mind spending thirty dollars for a pair of tights. To Ricky, maybe it was a larger investment than he could justify. Or maybe he had the money, and just didn't want to spend it. Even in high school he was known for his frugal ways.

Ricky simply shook his head.

*   *   *

Loup Loup Pass is the third of the five major climbs in Washington state. With some amount of confidence—I had, after all, survived the terror of Washington Pass—I set my sights on Dave, who was several hundred yards ahead of me on the climb.

On flat terrain, Dave and Ricky gradually distance themselves from me. No matter how hard I labor, I cannot keep up with Ricky's youthful vigor, or Dave's muscular legs. On uphill climbs, though, Dave's speed slows—he pays a premium for the extra pounds of gear. I catch him almost immediately, but slow my speed to match his. I'd rather have the company than to always be by myself. Ricky rarely slows his speed, but rather is intent on maintaining his own pace. On this climb, we suspected he was almost a half hour ahead of us, if the roadside revelers were to be believed.

"You guys better get your act together. You'll never catch that babe at the pace you're going. She's at least twenty minutes ahead of you!"

Ricky, with his boyish physique and shaven legs had been mistaken for a woman. It was to be our last laugh of the day.

As we approached the summit, the volatile Washington weather once again turned nasty, as storm clouds raced in from the southeast. Bolts of lightening fired at the summit of Loup Loup. Dave and I slowed our speed, and watched in awe. Even with all our rain apparel, we had no desire to enter the fray. We stopped and watched until the storm passed, and then continued on to the summit.

But where was Ricky?

At the summit, we saw clues to what he must have experienced. Newly created ponds in the grassy meadows were testament to the intensity of the rain. Small limbs, spring leaves, and ice pellets scattered on the road provided further evidence of the storms intensity.

Ten minutes and five miles down from the summit, we found our friend. He was sitting on the wet ground, and stretching his left knee.

"I think I hurt my knee," Ricky said. "Did you get caught in that storm?"

Dave mentioned that we had slowed our speed, and missed the storm.

"I didn't have a choice. When I got to the top of Loup Loup, that's when I got hit with wind, rain and hail. The ice pellets were at least two inches in diameter. It was far worse than Washington Pass.

"The storm moved in so quickly I had no time to find shelter, so I continued to ride. The roads were wet, my glasses got fogged, and as a result, I couldn't control my bike. I prayed that no car would be coming the other way, because I was forced to use both lanes of the highway in an effort not to crash. I finally managed to stop by using my left leg and the brakes, but I twisted my knee."

As we examined his knee, Ricky began to shake—no doubt still chilled from the descent, but also due to his skimpy riding clothes. All he was wearing was a T–shirt and riding briefs. Rather than put warm clothes on, however, he got back on his bike and continued to ride.

About a half mile further down Loup Loup, we encountered a steep hill with enough pitch to get us back in our granny gears. Halfway up, Ricky stopped again and flexed his leg. I pulled alongside.

"My knee popped a second ago. There was a sharp pain, and then it went away. I guess my muscles are still too tight. I think I can ride, but I'm going to try to take it easy."

He walked his bike up the remainder of the hill, and then we all coasted into the Okanogan Valley. Bright blue skies and a warm sun rested our weary muscles as we rolled at over forty m.p.h. into Washington's apple country. Our long descent ended at the Western Restaurant in the town of Okanogan.

"Would you like to stop here and see a doctor?" I asked Ricky.

"No, I can make it," he replied. "Let's go."

Dave and I dutifully mounted our bikes, got back on Highway 20 and began the twenty–four mile ride to Tonasket. This time, Ricky was content to ride behind us, and take advantage of the "draft" position. Dave consistently checked his bike odometer—we didn't want to go too fast, and push our young friend. Still, from looking at Ricky, I could tell he was in pain. His mouth was set in a tight grimace, and his shoulder and neck muscles were tense from the stress of the injury. He didn't complete full cycles with his left leg, near the bottom of the extension he would stop the motion, and let his right leg carry the load.

Half way to Tonasket, he began to whistle "Colonel Bogey," the theme song from the movie "The Bridge over the River Kwai."

"That's not a very happy movie," I noted.

"Every time I'm in pain, I whistle that song," he said. "I think of the prisoner that was locked up in the hothouse. He had it tough. A twisted knee is nothing when compared with real pain."

The youthful sins of pride and arrogance combined to twist Ricky's knee. Maybe the positive qualities of youthful enthusiasm, and physical resilience will allow Ricky to complete the trip.

Not Guilty, Your Honor

Afoot and light–hearted, I take to the open road,
Healthy, free, the world before me,
The long brown path before me leading wherever I choose.
Henceforth I ask not good–fortune, I myself am good fortune,
Henceforth I whimper no more, postpone no more, need nothing,
Done with indoor complaints, libraries, querulous criticisms,
Strong and content, I travel the open road.

—Walt Whitman,
Song of the Open Road

Possibly in sympathetic response to Ricky's injury, my right knee began to ache. It doesn't surprise me, during my conditioning program, which consisted of daily runs, Nautilus exercises, and weekend bike rides, my knees and ankles occasionally inflamed, and I would be forced to rest for several days. The human body, or at least the human body of a tall, skinny redhead, isn't designed for this type of abuse.

Arriving in Tonasket, we searched for the dreaded campground. By now, Ricky was not even bothering with "Colonel Bogey." His teeth were clinched in agony, as we circled the town in search of a place to stay. We received one offer from a local apple farmer.

"I've seen you boys on the road for three days now, and I figure I can trust you. I've been out tacking up bulletins around the county for an upcoming bluegrass festival. You guys have sure put in a lot of miles. Feel free to camp in my apple orchard if you like."

I thought about the offer.

"Well, if you've seen us for three days, you know that we've been rained on, snowed on, and hailed on. You also know that we're hungry and tired, and that Dave and I hate to camp. Our buddy Ricky is in complete agony, and may need a major operation. In this three day period you've seen us, we've yet to commit a serious crime. So the least you can do is fix us a hot dinner, offer us steaming showers, and apologize for the crummy Washington weather."

I really didn't say that, but that is what I was thinking.

I really said, "Thank you for your kind and generous offer. We may be back."

Back in town, a waitress in an ice cream restaurant directed us to a youth hostel that had just opened. I wasn't sure what a hostel was, but I was sure it wasn't a campground. And that was all that mattered. Dave gave me the details as we cycled the short distance.

A youth hostel is an inexpensive, dormitory style accommodation for travelers of all ages. Prices range from four to twelve dollars per night—the exact price depends on the number of services (breakfast, dinner, laundry, etc.) that are available. Membership in the hostel network is required, but non-members can purchase a guest card for three dollars per night. There are hundreds of these hostels across the country.

John and Joy, the managers of the hostel, greeted us as if we had guaranteed reservations. Ten minutes after we arrived, we were treated to an excellent dinner. The most enjoyable part of the hostel, however, was being in a heated home, with real sofas, chairs, and beds. Our first three days have been brutal, I thought, as I relaxed in heated comfort for the first time since the trip began. I propped my own sore right knee on the coffee table, and listened as all discussed Ricky's injury.

"Maybe your knee is just tight and will loosen up in the morning," offered Joy.

"Some rest might do it good," Dave volunteered, "maybe if you can stay off your bike a day or two, it'll be better."

Perhaps John had the best advice. "There's a hospital in town, and there will be a doctor on call tomorrow. Go down, have it checked out, and then make a decision."

Conversations about Ricky's knee went on for at least an hour. I listened for a while, and then became preoccupied with my own thoughts.

What if the doctor tells Ricky that if he rests for a week, he will be able to continue the trip?   What should Dave and I do? We don't have the luxury of time. Would it be fair to Ricky, though, to leave him behind?

I became absorbed with the internal conflict. Yes, I needed a courtroom to hear all of the arguments. That might help, perhaps a wise, learned, judge would proceed over the hearing.

"Quiet!" I screamed. I didn't get just one judge, I got three. All were properly identified, though—small brass plaques displayed their names. But why three? And why were there so many spectators?

This wasn't what I wanted at all. This was a kangaroo court, not a judicial hearing.

Court was in order, and for some inextricable reason, all three judges were reading their verdicts at the same time. "You lady, the nun, you go first," I commanded. I wasn't going to let this hearing get out of control.

"I want you to know, Bill, that Ricky is not your responsibility. He's an adult, and capable of making his own decisions."

"I salute your opinion, Mother Superior," I said. "Absolutely right, not my fault." At this, the smiling nun executed a smart curtsy, and exited right. Briefly, I became engrossed with the title of "Mother Superior," but then decided not to dwell on the possibilities, and instead, I turned my attention to the second judge.

"Father Time, read your verdict, and be quick about it." I gave this order to the far left judge, the one dressed in clergical garb.

"What's the hurry, my son? Ah, so you may have to wait seven whole days. Ricky is still young and may need your help. He is your buddy and your friend. You should not underestimate the importance of friendship. Let us spend more time on this subject. Now the apostle Peter once said...

"Stop!" I shouted. "I don't want to hear it. And I don't have the time to discuss the issue. Exit right, sir." Several spectators in the courtroom were pleased at my response, and stomped their feet.

"Order! Order!" snarled the middle judge. A hush fell on the crowd.

The third judge had not yet presented his front to the courtroom. Dressed in a gray suit, and smelling of Old Spice cologne, I could tell that he was used to respect.

"Now please, sir, be quick, what's your verdict?" I asked.

"No. You plead your case, Mr. Bill. Only then will I rule."

I cleared my throat. "Very well, your Honor."

"It was his decision to pedal alone, far ahead of his riding companions."

"It was his decision to pedal through the violent storms, instead of slowing down and finding shelter."

"It was his decision to not buy tights."

"I rest my case, your Honor." My crisp, well–presented arguments did not go unnoticed. Once again, my supporters stomped on the floor.

"Silence, fools," ordered the judge. Without turning around, he then delivered a sharp blow to my conscience.

"Don't wash your hands so quickly. You should have insisted that young Ricky, literally and figuratively, follow your lead."

With this pronouncement, the judge evaporated into the curtains. I turned for moral support from the gallery, but they too had gone; only a few boxes of popcorn, a couple of Cokes, and one old copy of *People* magazine were evidence of their attendance.

Slowly exiting the courtroom was a man dressed in black robes. Haven't I seen him before? Wasn't he on that Alaskan Air flight? Why is he shaking his head?

Jay & Linda

*I would have every man rich
that he might know the worthlessness of riches.*

—Emerson

Jay is almost a legend in the state of Washington. He goes to great lengths, we were told, to get cyclists to stay in his hostel. We were warned early and often, yet here we were, soaking in his hot tub.

The tub is the ultimate weapon in Jay's arsenal. People from miles away told us that in particularly foul weather, Jay gets in his pickup and goes fishing for cyclists. I grinned, visualizing the scene. The poor cyclist, tormented by rain, sleet, and snow; struggles against a growing desire to stop. And then, poof! A demon offering a dry house and a steamy hot tub shows up to torment him further. I suspect that many cyclists glance over their shoulder, and then toss their bikes onto the pickup, ducking down slightly to avoid being seen by the "You Didn't Bike All the Way Across the Country" authorities.

Jay's trickery started at the Tonasket hospital this morning.

"Ricky's not going to be able to bicycle for a few days. He'll need a ride to our youth hostel next town over. My wife's driving to Spokane on Wednesday. He can stay with us 'till then and rest his knee, and then he can ride down in the car and catch up with you guys. I even have a hot tub at my place. C'mon, let's go."

Jay had interrupted the doctor's examination of Ricky's knee. We didn't expect to see Jay here, for while we had made reservations for his hostel last night, we had no particular reason to suspect he'd show up at the Tonasket hospital.

The doctor looked at Jay as if to say, "Who the hell are you, and why are you interrupting me?" Instead, he said nothing, and continued to study the X-rays and test the flexibility of Ricky's knee.

"Your knee needs rest," he told Ricky. "I think you've suffered a deep bruise, one that will take time to heal. Perhaps in a couple of days you'll be well enough to cycle, but in the meantime, I'm going to prescribe an isotonic exercise program and some muscle relaxant medication. I think 400 mg. of Motrin will be sufficient."

This news was encouraging. Maybe in a few days Ricky will be at full strength, and able to continue. Today, though, Jay will give Ricky a ride over to his hostel in Republic, and Dave and I will meet him there this afternoon.

*   *   *

It was an uneventful trip over Wauconda Pass until we arrived in Republic, which is near Jay's hostel, and I had a flat tire—an aggravating experience that is quickly becoming a daily routine.

"Here, throw your bike in the back, I have a bike rack at the hostel, you can fix it there." I should have known Jay would appear. He had come into town for a few groceries. This guy is everywhere! So much for pedaling every mile of the trip. I tossed my bike onto the pickup and settled in for the ride to the hostel.

"Not a bad place guys," I said as I joined Dave and Ricky who had already settled into Jay's famous hot tub. My friends agreed, and for a few minutes we enjoyed the view. Off to the left were a couple of barns, a tractor and some other farm equipment. A few horses and cows shared a pasture which was enclosed by a well–kept, brown board fence. Mountains circled Jay's land, and marked the end of the property.

Surprisingly, in several weeks, Jay and his wife, Linda, will be leaving this picturesque setting and relocating their hostel to Kalispell, Montana. It is their hope that they will pick up more year–round visitors. The cyclists in the summer will still come, and by virtue of their proximity to several ski areas, they hope to snag some winter visitors as well.

Jay and Linda, in addition to their hostel responsibilities, are both teachers in Republic. Both are in their late forties, and are avid cyclists. While Linda prepared beef stew and biscuits for dinner, we learned more of their plans.

"Jay and I will really miss this place," she said. "We've been here over five years and have met a lot of nice people. We think we can make more money in Kalispell, though. Maybe we won't have to work as hard up there. It would be nice, at our age, to slow down just a little. "Did Jay tell you that we used to love to ride our bicycles together?"

"Yes," I said. Dave and I had noticed their Cannondales in the barn. From the cobwebs around the wheels, it looked as though they hadn't been used in a while.

Linda continued, "Lately we've been so busy, we just haven't had time to ride. When we move to Kalispell, Jay and I hope to find the time to start taking bicycle tours again. It's something that we really enjoy doing together."

Dinner was enjoyable, and the time passed quickly, as Jay and Linda regaled us with tales of previous guests. After helping clean up, we went back to our room. In a few minutes, Jay came back to settle our account.

"Let's see. First we have dinner. I'm not quite sure what to charge you. I usually charge either $2.75, or $3.00, depending on the type of dish. Let me check with Linda." He reappeared in a few minutes. "The dinner will be $2.75.

"Now about the hostel. We charge $8.00 per person, and that includes your hot tub and use of the bike racks. That makes the total for each of you $10.75." Perhaps he was disconcerted with the alacrity in which Dave and I paid. He began to lecture us about money.

"What kind of budget are you guys on?" he asked.

Budget was something that Dave and I had discussed in general terms. I told Ricky what I thought it would cost—I'm not sure he believed me though.

"Twenty-five dollars a day!" I blurted.

"Forty dollars!" said Dave.

"Twelve dollars!" said Ricky.

Jay was comfortable with Ricky's answer, so he turned his attention to Dave and me. "You guys are going about this all wrong," he said. "You should do this trip on ten dollars a day."

I thought about this for a minute.

"Hell, Jay, you just charged me $10.75, I can't afford tomorrow!" He didn't hear me.

"Your first mistake is the big meals that you're eating. You need to snack during the day, and cook spaghetti at night."

I had a flashback to the peanut butter sandwiches on the climb to Rainy Pass. "Wait a minute," I said, "that isn't right at all. You can't cycle across this country on peanut butter sandwiches. You've got to eat at least three hot meals a day." Jay didn't seem to hear me. He continued.

"Now you're probably camping at fancy campgrounds. Let me help you out with that."

He then wrote down a slew of public parks, along with strategic contacts.

"These folks," he said, "work at the public swimming pools. If you slip them fifty cents or a dollar, they will let you use the showers."

I pondered that one for a while. It just didn't sound like me.

"With your plan, Jay," I replied, "there is no way we could finish the trip. I'd end up losing twenty pounds, I wouldn't sleep, and I'd be nabbed by the local police for bribing an underage minor. The only good part of your plan is I would have enough money left over to make bail!"

Even Jay laughed at this.

"When do you guys plan on finishing?" Jay inquired.

"Six weeks," Dave said.

Jay shook his head emphatically. "No way," he said. "It can't be done. You might as well plan to ride to St. Louis and fly home from there."

After he left, Ricky, Dave, and I continued to talk about budgets. Dave and I now believe that three square meals and a warm bed are a daily necessity. Ricky is equally convinced that peanut butter and sleeping on dirt is the only way to go. We will have to strike a happy medium if we are to remain a harmonious group.

*   *   *

On Monday, Dave and I say good–bye to Jay and Linda. We also say good–bye to Ricky. In two days, we hope to catch up with him at Round Lake State Park in Idaho. Linda will give him a ride to Spokane, and Ricky will have to take it from there.

I feel strange leaving Ricky behind. The old bulls will continue the journey, while the rippling adolescent faces an uncertain future. If the young buck had been anybody but Ricky, Dave and I might be given to warm glows of satisfaction—it's always fun to see experience triumph over youth. There is no pleasure, though, in seeing such a fine person as Ricky being dealt such a difficult lesson.

*   *   *

Dave and I stopped for breakfast at a small cafe, not too far from the youth hostel. The "double breakfast" has now become our standard order—a loaded omelet and pancakes, and yes ma'am, we want the buttered toast that comes with the eggs.

For one of the few times to date, we had a relaxing moment to talk about the trip. Dave, though, had been doing some serious thinking.

"Jay has a valid point about budgets, but I really didn't come on this trip to see how much money I could save. I'd almost rather stay at home than have to worry about it. Heck, this is a once–in–a–lifetime opportunity. We may never become rich, but we can always look back and say we did this. Something to talk about when we're old and gray and sitting around the fireplace.

I agreed with Dave's sentiments. I, too, don't want to be eighty and saying, "Boy, I wish I had done that."

"Bill, I had been out of college five years before I realized the only person holding me back in life was myself. I had just started a new job in California, and found myself at a crossroads. I could continue, just going along and reacting to whatever happened, or I could try something new, maybe take charge and make a few decisions on my own. With a clean slate, I kept a record of how I spent my time. I also sent a progress report to my boss every week. After about six weeks, my new boss called me into his office. I was sure he was going to scream at me for leaving early the day before. Instead, he thanked me for my extra efforts, told me I had excellent potential, and gave me a bonus on top of that. I was shocked."

"That's great," I said. "I've never had any boss tell me I had potential."

"One success led to another, and after only seven years, I was the manager of the engineering department, and married to a beautiful woman with a fine fourteen–year–old stepson. A success by anyone's definition.

"Two years later, things changed. Downsizing eliminated my department and I was shuffled from one assignment to another with fewer opportunities for advancement. I knew I had to do something to handle the stress. My good friend, Tom Lagatta, had been bugging me to bicycle with his group. I took him up on his offer, and found that not only did it relieve the stress, but it was something I really enjoyed. Especially the challenge of long distance touring. Then, as you know, I got divorced. After all my efforts, I found myself back in an apartment just like the one I had out of college."

I had heard enough. "Dave, I don't want to say we've been here too long, but the lunch crowd is beginning to come in."

Dave continued anyway. "I guess what I'm trying to say, is that some things, like budgets, are right for some people at some time in their life. But right now, I feel like I've spent enough of my life on a budget. It's time to splurge. You know, order the eggs benedict once in a while, with the extra sauce."

"Enough, Dave, we have a big day planned, and we need to get moving." Engineers can get easily caught up in their own details. I couldn't bear to watch this happen.

Dave was slightly perturbed that I interrupted his stream of consciousness, but it was time to get back on the bikes. Ahead of us was Sherman Pass, which is the last major climb in Washington state. There is also the outside possibility that we will catch some fellow cyclists. Jay had informed us that two days prior to our arrival, another group of three had spent the night in his hostel.

"You boys will probably catch 'em today," he had informed us before we left this morning.

That didn't seem likely at all.

"Never happen," I said, "Dave and I aren't even averaging thirteen miles per hour in these hills. You're crazy if you think we can catch up to other cyclists in one day. Nope, not a chance."

"I think you will," he said, "there is something different about this group."

Honeymooners

Be Like the Bird, who
Halting in his Flight
On Limb too slight
Feels it give way beneath him,
Yet sings,
Knowing he hath wings.

—Victor Hugo,
Be Like the Bird

Late in the afternoon, Dave and I called it a day, and wheeled our bikes into Beaver Lodge Resort. In the morning, we had climbed Sherman Pass. It was a scenic ride until we reached the ten thousand burned acres near the top of the pass. A sign informed us that this was the result of a discarded match. The afternoon ride wasn't nearly as pleasant, however; the terrain was challenging, and once again we were chilled by intermittent showers. When we learned that our cabin had a fireplace, we knew we had made the right decision. On the way to our cabin, a fellow cyclist greeted us.

"Hi guys!" A pleasant looking woman poked her head out of a cabin window. She was still wearing her biking gloves.

"Come on over and get some chili!" A second woman issued the invitation—she had popped her head out of another window. She was joined at the window by a third person, a clean cut guy with short blonde hair. He didn't exhibit quite the same enthusiasm as the women, though. While they both possessed wide, easygoing smiles, he appeared slightly sullen; perhaps it had been a difficult day on the bike. Three was the magic number, though, this must be the group that Jay had mentioned.

But how did we catch these people? Dave and I had ridden less than eighty miles today, and the threesome, according to Jay, had a two day head start. Nobody appeared hurt, and all seemed cheerful enough.

"Let's get to the bottom of this!" I said to Dave. Armed with a six pack of Heineken, ice cold from the lodge's store, we walked down a small, well-trodden path to meet our fellow cyclists.

The door opened.

Dave and I knew immediately why we had caught these people in only one day. There's no easy, polite way to say it. The women, while having pretty features, also had...

Huge bottoms.

Two guys were also in the room. We had already seen the first—in contrast to the women, however, he was in excellent shape, with little fat on his six–foot frame. The second was also in good shape, and had the easy, confident air of someone used to making himself at home. All members of this curious contingent appeared to be in their late twenties.

"Er, you both look alike," I commented to the two women. "In the face, you know."

"We're sisters," one explained. "My name is Chris, and this is Caroline. You saw my husband, Jeff, at the window. We all met Tom today—he was cycling by himself and decided to join us. I hope you guys missed the storm that came up an hour or so ago. Rather than battle through it, we decided to quit early and relax."

Dave and I shook hands with all. Chris continued.

"Jeff and I are on our honeymoon. We always talked about taking a long bike tour together, so when we decided to get married, we realized that it might be special if we also realized another dream, and that is to bike across the country. We started a couple of weeks ago, and hope to finish up in Jamestown, Virginia, where my parents live, in a couple of months."

Chris continued to talk, but I wasn't paying too much attention. On their honeymoon with her sister? It wasn't a question of separate cabins, either. I counted beds and bikes. Two beds and four bikes in this tiny fifteen by fifteen room. OOPS! What was the fourth bike doing in here. I glanced at Tom and Caroline—what fast friends they had become. Who said that plain old hospitality is gone from America.

"How did you ever make it up Washington Pass?" Dave asked.

"It wasn't easy," said Chris, "it took us all day, and sometimes we felt we weren't going to make it. But we stuck with it. The view from the top was outstanding. We had a warm, sunny day—nothing at all like what you guys went through—and we could see for miles."

Chris did all the talking for the group. Occasionally her sister chimed in with a comment or two, and Tom also added a few thoughts. Jeff was silent, and had nothing to say. He listened to the conversations, and once in a while offered a nervous smile. Mostly, he was content to fidget with a few bike accessories.

I asked them how many miles they had been averaging.

Chris answered for the group. "So far, we are averaging about forty miles per day, but we hope to build up to sixty or seventy. We started training for this last fall, but the weather back home didn't cooperate, so instead of riding, we did a lot of training in the gym. I wish we could have ridden more—both Caroline and I put on some extra weight, but we did the best we could."

She added the last comment with a wide smile. It's obvious that she is perfectly comfortable "being herself," and if that means a few extra pounds, so be it. You can't help but admire that kind of attitude.

Tom spoke up. "I'll probably ride a week or so with my new friends, and then head south towards Kansas. I have some friends that live in the state. I started out in Seattle, with no real destination in mind. After eight years as a stock broker, I wanted to do something different."

Different he got. Three weeks ago he was working in front of a computer terminal, selling stocks, options, and other pieces of paper, and today, near the small town of Ione, Washington, he is sharing a cabin with three people that he met just this morning.

Dave asked Jeff about his previous trip across the country.

"We went across the central part of the country," he said. "I liked Colorado the best. It took us about seven weeks. It was a great experience. When I told Chris about my first trip, she told me that someday it might be fun to take a long trip together, but I was still surprised when she suggested it for our honeymoon."

I wanted to ask Jeff the obvious question, "How did you feel when she brought her sister along?"

Instead, I said "It's great that you all got to take this trip together."

We talked for a few more minutes, and then Dave and I strolled back to our cabin, the remaining Heinekins in hand.

What credit they deserve! While Dave and I know our trip will not be easy, we both realize that theirs will be that much more difficult. Or will it? If you have the desire to accomplish a goal, what difference does it make if it takes you a bit longer? What difference does it make if you don't quite "look the part" for an endeavor? Is that a good reason not to make the effort? Isn't it better to say you participated, as opposed to just watching and wishing?

Dave had his own thoughts.

"I think that you make your own choices in life. Doors are always opened if you have the right attitude. But you have to believe that things will work out for the best. This attitude creates opportunities and "opens doors" where none should be expected. I call this the "Corridor Effect.""

Engineers are like that. Every thought has a label, every label a compartment, and every compartment shares a box. Salesmen just have one big bucket that fits everything.

Dave continued. "Regardless of how things may seem at the moment, I believe the Corridor Effect will cause things to eventually work out for the best. Cynics say that this theory is a cheap trick that keeps a person from facing reality, but I think there is more to it. If the honeymooners believe they can make it, then they will prevail. Who knows, by the end of their trip they may even lose a few pounds."

*   *   *

I have made it a point to call home as often as possible to talk with Leith and Molly. Though Leith never says anything, I can almost hear the relief in her voice when I call and inform her that I have survived yet another day without being mashed by a logging truck, or taken off into the woods by some outlaw gang, looking just like the toothless hillbillies in the movie *Deliverance*.

Our conversations are usually about the experiences of the day. I tell Leith about the number of miles traveled, or describe some of the people we met and places we have visited. Leith tells me about her day, and to her credit, her responses are almost uniformly positive. She has yet to complain about a "long day with Molly," or about the stress and pressure of being a lone parent, even if only for a short time. I'm thankful she hasn't given into the temptation. If she said, for example, "life is hell and I need you back here," I would head straight home, but I think there would be resentment. I feel we have responsibilities to ourselves as well as our spouses, and to give in to either one would not be good. While considering these matters, I wandered down the path to the phone by the main office to make my nightly call. I was not quite all the way through the story of the honeymooners, when Leith interrupted me.

"Do you miss me Bill?" she asked.

I paused before answering—it really wasn't a simple question.

"Yes, and no," I responded. I think she understood.

I do love my wife. But this journey, and the motivation for the journey, are mine. I am doing what I've always wanted to do, and for a little while, nothing else matters. I think most of us crave for periods where responsibility is absent, and we do what we want. How much resentment is stored when this is not the case? How many times have childhood dreams vanished, the dreamy adolescent desires disappearing as easily as quarters in a slot machine? How many times do we all say, "If I had only..."

"I'm glad you're having a good time," she said, with no discernible hint of frustration. "By the way, are you still searching for your lost soul?" There was a just a hint of sarcasm in that one.

"Well, yes," I responded.

Leith always eyed me suspiciously when I told her of my desire to search for my lost soul. I don't blame her for this, my buddies all did the same. My wife is a very spiritual person, and takes discussions of the soul quite seriously. It's too bad she didn't have the chance to attend Sister Mary William's first grade class in religion. She would have learned that a soul weighs about an ounce, gets dirty when you lie, and can be scrubbed clean when you go to confession. Once you accept all of that, the rest is easy.

Actually, in fairness to Leith's question, I have been giving the matter some thought. What if I can't find the real America, or worse, discover The CBS Evening News is right, that there is nothing but bad news to talk about? What if the trip turns out to be like work, where a mile becomes no different than an hour at the office? What if after all of this, I don't recapture my soul?

I got another problem, too. I'm not sure that it would do me much good to find my soul so early in the trip. There would be no reason for the rest of the trip, and it would be time to go home. I shuddered, though, as I played the scene through. My skeptical, Benedict Arnold–type friends would all have a celebration on my return.

"Why we're so glad you found your soul, Bill," they would say, with sarcasm spewing like snake venom. "Naturally, we never dreamed, however, that you would find it so early in the trip. Of course, we know you wouldn't have returned so suddenly because you were worn out, and couldn't pedal another mile!" I would then be the recipient of toasts such as "To Bill, one who found his soul 2500 miles west of New Bern, North Carolina, and then quit."

I said good–bye to Leith, stomped back to the cabin, and told Dave we needed to get an early start in the morning.

*   *   *

Today will be our last day in Washington. We will cross into Idaho this afternoon and meet Ricky at Round Lake State Park. It should be a beautiful ride—most of the time we will be cycling in view of the Pend Oreille River.

Lost Souls

Stranger, if you passing meet me and desire to speak to me, why
should you not speak to me?
And why should I not speak to you?

—Walt Whitman,
To You

I knew the third judge's words would haunt me. Characters often come back to me unannounced—they never have the courtesy to phone ahead, and let me know of their plans. They often snake in through the back door, slither around the house, and quietly tiptoe to some cob–webbed nook in the living room, patiently awaiting the occasion to reappear with a moral judgment, or perhaps a knowing nod of the head.

The judge was right. I should have taken Ricky's youth and inexperience into account, and insisted on more of a team approach. I was guilty of assuming that Ricky was experienced enough to make the correct decisions. It is easy to look at him and see a physically strong, incredibly bright, moral person, and not see a twenty–one year old kid.

Dave and I made it on schedule at 5:00 p.m. to Round Lake State Park. But where was Ricky? We circled the campground and examined all the campsites hoping to catch a glimpse of our young friend. No Ricky.

Should I call his parents and give them the news? Should I call the police? For close to an hour Dave and I discussed our options. Shortly before 6:00 p.m., though, the issue was resolved.

"Special delivery! That'll be a hundred and fifty dollars," the lady said.

She was an employee of the Postal Service and was driving an official vehicle. Still, that's a lot of money to pay for a delivery.

"No ma'am," I joked. "We refuse the charges. Return to sender."

Anne, the postal employee, pulled into our campsite, and delivered one Ricky Borry. I looked carefully—there weren't any stamps on his forehead. How did he get here? It didn't take us long to find out. Ricky was one wound–up fellow.

"After you guys left the youth hostel, I sanded and stained two bunk beds for Jay. He told me that in return for the work, he would knock a few dollars off of my bill. That job kept me busy for a few hours, and helped keep my mind off my injury. Every few minutes, though, I stretched and tested my knee to see if there was any improvement, but there wasn't. I knew then I would have to take them up on their offer to drive me to Spokane, and then hitchhike from there."

A slight smile crossed my lips. Even as a freshman in high school, Ricky always stayed busy finding ways to earn money, or figuring ways to save money. Often he went to the extreme. One memorable time, his friends in the high school church youth group torched the only pair of sneakers he had brought to a six day retreat. They were smelly, old shoes with holes worn through from his toes. They thought if was high time for a new pair, even if Ricky didn't.

I suppose the frugal behavior is easily explained. His parents are children of Christian missionaries and were raised with minimal material luxuries. Thriftiness and economy were absolute requirements, and they have passed these traits on to their children. Even now, Ricky's dad, Dick, takes great pride in "showing off" the old beaten up Dodge Dart he salvaged from "death by crushing." Mom and Dad also instilled Christian love in their children.

Ricky continued. "Late that afternoon, Linda and I drove into Republic to run some errands. While there, Linda told me the real reason they were moving. Remember we couldn't figure out why they would leave such a beautiful place? A couple of months ago, a bomb exploded in their front yard. It could have killed them both. The police found out it was made and planted by a fifth grader at school. Rather than treat this as a serious crime, the townspeople dismissed it as a prank.

"It was sad in town. So many people came up and wished Linda well. When we got back to the hostel, I helped them pack.

"The next day, Linda gave me a lift to Spokane. I unloaded my bike from the truck, strapped on my helmet, and rode all of a city block before being forced to quit. The pain was too much. I knew then I had to hitchhike if I was to catch up with you guys here at Round Lake."

I've never hitchhiked or even picked up a hitchhiker before. I was brought up to never do such things. What kind of people did Ricky meet?

"I managed to walk my bike to a gas station just outside the city. I was sure that a truck driver would give me a ride to Newport. Finally, a construction worker named Steve gave me a lift. I thought he said he was going to Newport, but he turned off, so I only went ten miles with him.

"Another guy stopped and asked if I was in trouble. I explained the situation, but he said he had a new truck, and didn't want to scratch the truck bed with my bike. He did wish me luck, though. That was nice, but Jesus said, give the guy your coat, don't just say 'May God take care of you.' I sure hope I remember to bend over backwards for people in need."

Ricky is an exceptional person. When other people might get discouraged, and curse and swear, Ricky tries to learn from the experience.

"Another fellow, Larry, gave me a ride to the Ram Drive-In, which is twenty miles south of Newport. Larry is an alcoholic, but he quit drinking on February 19th. He's on unemployment now, but used to work in a steel mill. He doesn't think he'll go back since the job's too hard. His wife works as a coffee salesman.

"Funny thing. I sat on the road with my "ride wanted" sign for over an hour. Half the people looked, half ignored me, and one stopped but couldn't help. Larry, who looked like the last guy in the world to stop and help, did his best.

"Sam, who lives in Riverside, gave me a lift for a few miles. For a while, I thought he was the true good Samaritan. But at Newport he said, 'I'll take you all the way, but not for nothing. I'll do it for twenty bucks, though.' That sort of destroyed his image."

I didn't say anything to Ricky, but I know what I would have said if Sam had made me the same offer.

"Is that all? What a deal for such a special service. Here let me give you forty dollars, I'd really feel much better."

Did frugality prevent Ricky from doing this? Or was he truly trying to find the Good Samaritan? At what point should all of us accept, or at least acknowledge, the realities of the world? Or should we refuse this tacit approval of the ordinary, and inform others of our higher expectations?

"Finally, I stopped at the Athol post office to mail a letter. They had just closed, but two ladies opened the door and let me in. I told them what I was doing and asked for directions to the park. Anne offered to give me a ride here—an offer I gladly accepted. I didn't relish another hour or so of one–legged riding."

I guess not.

Talk died out after Ricky finished his stories. His injured knee will prevent him from cycling for at least a few more days. His attitude amazes me; I know I would be devastated if I could not continue this trip. Yet, he seems almost tranquil in his outlook. He talks of the interesting people he has met, and the interesting people he has yet to meet. There is no bitterness in his voice, no disgust, no "if I had only" reproaches.

My reaction would be quite different.

*   *   *

In the morning, Dave made another one of his excellent meals, and we then took leave of our young friend. Our plan is to now catch up with him at Glacier National Park, which is three to four hundred miles from Round Lake. He will once again depend on rides to get there—a fact that deeply troubles me.

"Check the bus lines," I told Ricky. "Sandpoint is only a few miles from here, go to the Greyhound station there, buy a ticket, and get to Glacier ahead of us. This will give your knee plenty of time to rest, and perhaps you'll be able to continue the journey. I'd feel better if you did that, I really don't want you hitching anymore."

I don't think he is going to follow my advice. I walked down to a pay telephone by the front office and called his parents.

"Look," I told Margaret and Dick, "I really don't feel good about this. It is my suggestion that when Ricky calls you, that you tell him to return home. The next several days we will be traveling through some desolate country, and I'd just as soon Ricky not be by himself."

Am I paranoid? My mom and dad raised me to have a healthy skepticism of strangers. I have never forgotten all of their admonitions about candy, strangers, and hitchhiking. As an adult, all I have to do is turn on the television, or read the paper, and I'm quickly reminded of the soundness of their advice. My dad even wanted me to pack a gun for this trip, and I did consider his suggestion.

Dick and Margaret listened, but decided to leave the final decision up to Ricky.

"He is twenty–one years old, Bill," Margaret said, "and he needs to make his own decisions. Dick and I accept the fact that our lives are in God's hands, and that we've got to believe in Him, and that He will judge, guide, and protect Ricky in his travels. It is a challenge to our faith to not worry, we've all got to believe in His love."

I do not doubt the sincerity of Margaret's words. A lifetime of prayer and study have gone into her beliefs, and she is trying not to be shaken with this trial.

As we talked, though, occasionally I heard words that were less confident. She is Ricky's mom, after all, and her injured son will shortly be thumbing rides into the Montana wilderness.

Hope

Old friends, Old friends,
Sat on their park bench like bookends.
A newspaper blown through the grass, falls on the round toes,
of the high shoes, of the old friends.
Can you imagine us years from today, sharing a park bench quietly?
How terribly strange to be seventy.

—Paul Simon,
Old Friends

After a scenic morning of cycling, Dave and I leaned our bikes against the outside of the Edelweiss Restaurant in Hope, Idaho. From Round Lake State Park, we cycled the entire morning along Lake Pend Oreille. Cool winds, and frequent rain, whipped at the water, occasionally causing us to put on additional clothing. Our only disappointment was in not seeing any moose—we noted many "Beware of Moose" signs.

I limped into the restaurant behind Dave, once again my right knee was hurting. The injury doesn't prevent me from completing a full cycle on the bike, but when I sit down for a few minutes, it tightens up. I am hoping that the stress of the long climbs in Washington have caused the problem, and if I can make it out of the hills and into the plains—we are probably a week away—then the demands on my knee will lessen.

Dave and I plopped our sore bodies into the comfortable black leather seats at a table near the window. Despite being close to noon, we were the only diners in this fine, out–of–the–way restaurant. While Dave visited the men's room, I was left alone to my private thoughts.

There should be a woman here, I thought. I've had this fantasy ever since college; a secluded restaurant, much like this one, few if any other diners, and only an elderly waiter. He waits in the shadows, appearing only when a half–empty glass needs to be filled.

The woman I'm with is tall, elegant, and dressed in simple style—she is wearing a long white dress, cut closely to her neckline. A single gold chain wraps around her neck. Her high cheekbones, and trusting eyes speak of love, warmth and caring. We each sip on our vintage wine, knowing that in a few hours, we will be...

"Boy, I sure am hungry." My old buddy had returned.

It was all I could do to be civil.

*   *   *

Three elderly well–dressed women came into the restaurant while Dave and I were eating. They seemed curious about us, but were reluctant to break the ice and say "hello." Being a salesman, I'm used to taking the lead in these matters.

"I guess it's just us in the restaurant today," I noted.

They all nodded politely.

"Are you ladies from here?" I asked.

One of the three spoke up.

"Yes we are," she said. "While none of us live here now, we were all childhood friends in Hope. Marriage and careers took us away, but once a year, on this date, we get together to reminisce and catch up."

If they were childhood friends, and they are now in their mid-seventies, it meant that they grew up together, in this small, almost unnoticeable town, in the 1920's. What changes they must have seen—I asked them for some details.

"Hope is not the same anymore," the second woman said, "the small town feeling that we remember has given way to the tourist. When we lived here, there wasn't any of that. Hope was just a small town in Idaho, and if you didn't live here, there was no reason to stop for a visit. There certainly wasn't the development that you see today."

Dave and I politely nodded, but in truth, we hadn't seen much development at all. Sure, there were a few condominium projects along the shore, but forest, trees, and lakes still dominate the landscape. We had not yet seen a Marriott or McDonald's.

What do you do, during this day together, I asked. The first lady answered.

"Our tradition is the same. We always meet here for lunch, and usually spend a couple of hours talking—sometimes about old mutual friends, sometimes about the fun we had growing up, and sometimes about the people that are no longer with us.

"You boys are still pretty young, but when you get older, you will remember your friends and acquaintances that have passed away. After we have lunch, we always drive by our childhood homes, and talk about the people and events that we remember. When you get to be our age your perspective changes. The things that were serious and important then, and some of them seemed to be life and death at the time, are no longer as important.

"Our last hour or so is spent at the cemetery. We always pay respects to spouses and friends, because they are such an important part of our lives."

When she was telling us about the trip to the cemetery, the third lady turned her head and stared out the window.

"You boys are doing the right thing," the first lady noted. "Take the time to enjoy yourselves. All of us have had a good life, and we don't have many regrets. I think it's because each of us took on a challenge—whether it was a career, our hobbies, or the special challenge of being faithful to a spouse and raising a family."

When I looked again at Dave, this time I was pleased that he wasn't a seductive looking woman. I've always been able to depend on him. He's always lent a sympathetic ear to my irrational rambling, and I know I will treasure our friendship the rest of my life. These ladies reminded me that I should never take him for granted.

Then I thought about my gorgeous woman, and decided I would ditch Dave in a hurry.

"Are you guys pedaling on the main highway, or on the old highway?" the third lady wanted to know.

"Umm, I'm not really sure ma'am," I ventured.

"Stay on the highway closest to the mountains," the lady said, "it will take you through the town of Hope. You've already gone through East Hope, then you'll pass Hope, and then you'll go through the last town. We call it No Hope."

Dave and I followed their advice. Instead of pedaling the main highway along the lake, we rode on the pavement a few hundred yards inland. In truth, it wasn't worth the effort. We weaved back and forth on what was once the main road in order to avoid the sizable potholes. We're not sure we ever saw the town of Hope. Perhaps it was a couple of abandoned buildings that we passed, but we weren't sure.

We never did see the town of No Hope.

*   *   *

A few miles beyond Hope, we entered the state of Montana. We figure to be in this state awhile. The distance across is almost eight hundred miles.

Only an occasional car interrupted the solitude of the highway. The few stores and restaurants that we passed were closed. Maybe it's early in the tourist season, or maybe there just isn't a tourist season.

"I wouldn't want to be out in this country by myself," I told Dave during a break at a small crossroads store. While our bike maps indicated that a campground was nearby, all we saw was this single store. No gas station. No restaurant. Few people.

"Let's keep on moving, Bill. The bike maps show a couple more campgrounds down Highway 56."

"Just a minute, I want to see if Ricky has left us a message."

I found a pay phone and dialed my office voice mail system. I had given Ricky careful instructions on how to leave messages. I hung up the phone.

No message.

Dave and I got back on our bikes, made a left turn, and headed deeper into the Cabinet Mountains and the western Montana wilderness.

Part Three

Empty Shelves

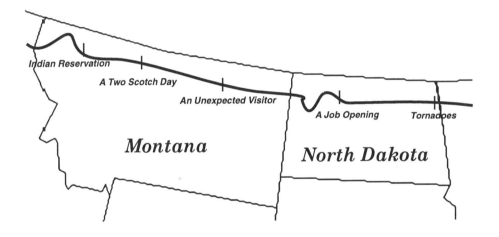

Indian Reservation

A Two Scotch Day

An Unexpected Visitor

A Job Opening

Tornadoes

Montana

North Dakota

Dave's Log			
Date	Miles	Destination	Day
5/30	77	Bull Lake, MT	8
5/31	98	Eureka, MT	9
6/1	53	Whitefish, MT	10
6/2	46	Apgar, MT	11
6/3	71	Essex, MT	12
6/4	102	Shelby, MT	13
6/5	44	Chester, MT	14
6/6	104	Harlem, MT	15
6/7	76	Saco, MT	16
6/8	115	Poplar, MT	17
6/9	78	Williston, ND	18
6/10	94	Parshall, ND	19
6/11	106	Towner, ND	20
6/12	105	Takota, ND	21

Scenery: ★★★★
The western one–third of Montana is to scenery what Picasso is to painting. Once you leave Glacier National Park, however, the scenery goes flat.

Roads: ★★★★
The traffic is light and the roads are wide with good shoulders. We had more flats in this area than any other. The reason? Little sharp stones are more plentiful than pickup trucks.

People: ★★★★★
Exceptional.

Weather: ★★★★★
Warm, breezy, and sunny. Only on one memorable day did the gods decide to toy with our emotions.

Alex & Eileen

*"Whether it's skiing in the winter, or fishing during the sum-
mer, you won't be disappointed at the Bull Lake Guest
Ranch! All year round you can find adventure, relaxation,
and that renowned Western Montana hospitality. It's all
here just waiting for you to discover it! Come and join us
for a vacation (or just for a weekend!) that won't soon be
forgotten!"*

Bull Lake Guest Ranch Brochure

When Dave and I turned left onto Montana Highway 56, we
entered a different sort of place. For close to an hour, not one car or
truck passed us on this lost, lonely highway. Yet, to describe the road
only in these terms would be unfair. When I gazed at the mountains,
and their images that reflected on the bordering lakes, I realized my own
insignificance, and that can be a lonely feeling. But this time, I did not
feel alone, for I also felt a spiritual presence. In my life, I have rarely had
these feelings, but it would be difficult to be on this highway, on a bicycle, and not feel so touched. For close to twenty miles, there were no
signs of life. No homes. No stores. No restaurants or gas stations. No
trash or billboards. What solitude! But what kind of people would live in
a place as remote as this? What would they be like? I mentioned all this
to Dave during a brief break, and found that he, too, was touched by the
area.

"This is God's country, Bill."

Still, you can carry this line of thought too far. "Let's see if God's
country has a bed for us tonight," I replied, as we got back on our bikes.

Dave and I stopped ever so briefly at the entrance to Bad Medicine campground. Long on weeds and short on people, we figured no
one with an option would stay there. Then too, we had seen numerous
"Bear Warning" signs in the area.

A few miles further down the road we came to a small community that borders on Bull Lake. The area offered no hope of lodging, or

even camping, until we noticed a weather–beaten sign that advertised a guest ranch. We wheeled our bikes into the gravel and dirt entrance, crested a hill, and came to a cleared area that contained a barn and several cottages. I opened the door labeled "Office."

The proprietor, Alex Thompson, gave us a warm welcome. A less gracious person might have turned us away, for it was the dinner hour, and Alex, his wife Eileen, and family were in the spacious living room enjoying coffee. A large wood stove in the corner was fully stoked and extended the same warmth and comfort as our hosts.

The rest of the living room exuded warmth and character as well. A huge bear skin rug hung over the couch, an elk rack supported a wide variety of cowboy hats, and a bobcat pelt hung on the wall by the corner. To complete the scene, everyone in the room wore sturdy boots, no nonsense jeans, and substantial flannels and wools.

Also hanging in a prominent spot on the wall was a plaque engraved with the second amendment to the Constitution. In large, bold letters, it read:

A WELL REGULATED MILITIA, BEING NECESSARY TO THE SECURITY OF A FREE STATE, THE RIGHT OF THE PEOPLE TO KEEP AND BEAR ARMS SHALL NOT BE INFRINGED.

Dave mentioned to Alex that he liked the plaque.

"Glad you do," he said. "I consider this to be one of our most important amendments. Many liberals would have all the common citizens turn over their guns to the government. Regular people would then have no way of defending themselves from a government takeover. Plus, a man has to be able to defend himself and his family from the common criminal."

I don't much care for guns at all, and feel that we need stricter controls. I've been in quite a few heated arguments with friends, like Alex, that take the same "protect ourselves from a government takeover" argument on gun control. When I hear the argument, it always conjures up the same image. A reporter, looking suspiciously like David Brinkley, is reporting from a "secure" place. In hushed tones, he informs us that the fate of the country is now in the hands of one brave American, who never surrendered his weapons to the government. This individual, looking like my Texan friend Greg Smith, flails away with a battery of handguns at the combined forces of the renegade Army, Air Force, and Navy. The embattled Smith's do just fine until the Special Forces are brought in, but even then, it takes another three hours to crush this brave family.

"I agree with most of what you say, Alex," Dave replied. "It's gotten so bad in Los Angeles, you have to depend on yourself for protection. But, I still don't own a gun. I guess I haven't gotten one because I like to think this is a more civilized world. I don't mind people owning guns, but things are out of control these days. I think it has to do with the breakdown in morality over the past twenty years."

"That's right," said Alex, "Eileen and I moved here from Pennsylvania almost thirty years ago for exactly those reasons. Things out here are different. God–fearing people live around these parts. We don't depend on the government for hand–outs or special privileges. Did you see the buildings out back? My family and I built them with our own hands.

"We live a simple life out here. You won't find us watching any television—fact is, we don't even own one. All our kids (and here he pointed at his adult children) we taught ourselves. We didn't send them to any government sponsored school to learn crazy ideas."

"It's just as well you don't bother with television," Dave said. "Today's programs are awful. I grew up watching The Walton's and Bonanza. Today, kids watch Beavis and Butthead."

Perhaps satisfied that Dave and I held viewpoints close to his own, Alex chatted a few more minutes about life in Montana, and after the conversation wound down, he led us outside, across the driveway to the comfortable guest house that was to be our home for the night. A casual glance of the carpeted rooms and queen–sized beds was enough to confirm the obvious—these accommodations are just a bit nicer than Bad Medicine campground.

*   *   *

Dave and I showered and hustled back to the main building. Eileen turned her kitchen over to Dave, and he wasted no time in preparing our dinner. Eileen joined me at the table.

"Alex won't be joining us tonight," she said, "he gets up early in the morning, usually finishes his work by dinner time, and then turns in for the night. In another few weeks, we will start our busy season. People from all over the country come to stay with us during the summer. In addition to helping with the guest ranch, I have a full time job

65

during the night shift at a local mine. When I get off work, I cook breakfast for the guests, fix their box lunches and then I go to bed. I wake up in time to cook dinner—sometimes fish they caught during the day—and then I go back to my full time job."

After dinner, Dave and I stood up to excuse ourselves. I grimaced as I attempted to extend my right leg. My right knee was the culprit, evidently the stresses of today were the final blow. The last few days I have noticed stiffness and increasing pain, but until today, I was able to avoid facing the truth. This is probably serious. I know I should see a doctor, but I don't want to hear his diagnosis. All he will do is tell me to go home and rest my knee. I don't want to hear that.

The scent of frying eggs and sausage, along with buttered hot cakes and freshly brewed coffee greeted us in the morning. We sat down and dug into our morning banquet. The talk turned to politics.

"A friend warned me about Jesse Jackson the other day," Alex said. "Did you know that if Jesse Jackson is elected president, he has promised every black slave descendent a hundred thousand dollars? Can you imagine that?" I said that I couldn't. I actually met Jackson a few months prior to our bike trip.

Jesse was in Greenville, visiting his mother and our paths crossed at the YMCA. As luck would have it, his locker was next to mine. I gave him a "Hello, Jesse." He gave me a watered–down grin and a limp handshake.

Alex took out a photo album and showed us his latest hunting pictures. I was still eating my runny eggs as he flipped through pages filled with pictures of big game hunters and dead animals. Ugghh. Breakfast and butchered animals really don't go well together. I smiled weakly, mumbled, "Oh, yes, very nice," several times, and tried to keep my food down. Mercifully, Alex ran out of pictures. Shortly after breakfast, Dave and I left.

During the morning ride, I thought about Alex and his family. Quiet, self sufficient, God–fearing people. In some quarters, people might consider them "John Birchers." This area suits their philosophy, I thought, as I gazed at the silent, desolate beauty of Montana.

*　　　　*　　　　*

U.S. Highway 2 will be our constant companion for the next several weeks as it traverses through the northern parts of Montana and

North Dakota. Today, though, when we pass Libby, we will temporarily leave this road and cycle instead on Highway 37 up by Libby Dam, and Lake Koocanusa. Our destination is Eureka, Montana.

The Road To Glacier

When a feller hasn't got a cent
And is feelin' kind of blue,
And the clouds hang thick and dark
And won't let the sunshine thro'
It's a great thing, oh my brethren,
For a feller just to lay
His hand upon your shoulder in a friendly sort o' way.

—Unknown

I stopped at the first pay phone we could find and called my brother–in–law, Bill Buice. He is a doctor back in South Carolina.

"I know how hard you've worked to prepare yourself for this trip," Dr. Bill said, "and you probably don't want to hear this. You should rest your knee. It is impossible to tell without an examination, but there is a possibility of permanent damage. If you decide to continue, ice your knee down every night and take some anti–inflammatory medicine. You probably won't quit, though, will you?"

"That's right, I'm not going to quit." I said. "This might be the only chance I'll ever have to bicycle across the country. I'm not going to stop just because of a sore knee." We talked a few more minutes, and then I hung up the phone.

Quit this trip? No way! For years I have dreamed of this opportunity, and to quit is simply not acceptable. I will follow Bill's advice, though, and get some Motrin and start icing my knee at night. Even if my body lets me down, I will make it to Glacier National Park, a distance of one hundred and seventy–five miles. During the year of preparation, I have often thought of this area, and how much fun it would be to ride the spectacular Going-to-the-Sun Highway. I even bought a poster that shows cyclists climbing up this magnificent roadway. When we completed the trip, we would all sign the poster, and I would have it as a permanent testament to desire, discipline, and friendship.

*　　　　*　　　　*

The ride from the Guest Ranch to Libby Dam was brutal. Road construction on U.S. 2 around Libby gave us the opportunity to ride on a smothering mixture of gravel, dirt, and loose concrete. Dust crept into every pore and orifice. Every time we sipped water, we manufactured mud. It was not a good start to what turned out to be a one–hundred mile day.

Around 2:00 p.m., we stopped for a lunch of broasted chicken and oven browned potatoes, and plotted our course to Eureka. The construction had put us way behind schedule, and we needed to cover seventy more miles to arrive at our destination. Our bike maps told us to expect little in the way of services along the next stretch of highway, but that the terrain was generally flat.

It was not. Scenic, yes. Flat, no. The highway, designed by the U.S. Army Corp of Engineers, displayed repetitive sameness. A ten minute "S" shaped climb, followed by a swooping "C" shaped two minute downhill. I had a sudden vision of a highway engineer designing the first mile of the highway, and then in a burst of bureaucratic ingenuity, duplicating the exact sketch forty times.

Of course, everything was getting on my nerves. My right leg was virtually useless, so I attempted to push up the hills using only my left leg. This proved to be impossible, so I had to endure sharp streaks of pain in my right leg on every pedal rotation. As bad as the physical pain was, the mental anguish was even worse. On the all–too–brief downhills, I looked ahead only to see more agony in the form of another climb. Dave was struggling too, and when we pulled into Libby Dam, we were in need of a break, a diversion, a change of scenery. And then we forgot all about our pain because out of nowhere, there appeared a...

Blonde.

Yes, we stared.

Our leggy six–foot blonde was wearing long black, red stripes–up–the–side tights, and an impressively tight tank top. Her long blonde hair curled around her neck, and rested gently on her, er, front.

After considerable thought, Dave came up with the first question.

"What are you doing here?"

69

In retrospect, it was a brilliant question. To me, it was every bit as impressive as the philosophical question about the tree falling in the forest.

"This is what I do in the summer to stay in shape," she said. While answering Dave's query, she had fished roller–blades out of the back of her yellow Volkswagen beetle. "I'm usually out here three to four times a week. What are you guys doing?"

I was pleased that Dave answered because I had forgotten exactly what we were doing.

"We're cycling across the country," he said, after some thought.

But that is all he could muster. And I still couldn't remember my name. With a shrug of her shoulders, our Libby Dam goddess skated into the distance. What a delightful distraction. Suddenly, my knee felt better. As if on reflex, we got back on our bikes and followed her out of the park. We did manage to return her wave as we passed her on the road to Eureka.

"Dave, I've got to tell you something. I've never so much as dated a blonde. All I ever dated was brunettes."

"Me too, Bill. Just brunettes."

We cycled the next fifteen miles in brooding silence.

*   *   *

Late in the day, we were again rewarded for our efforts. As we rounded another of the mind–numbing curves, our breath was taken away, not by a dam, or a blonde, but by the magnificent, surreal beauty of the snow capped Canadian Rockies. As if hypnotized, Dave and I both stopped cycling and stared open mouthed at the unmatched beauty. Tears came to my eyes—I'm not sure if they were because of the beauty, the suffering, or perhaps the realization that if I made it no further, I would never forget the sight. Not even an old steel bridge across the Kootenai River could mar the image. If anything, its paltry frame paled next to the natural beauty, as if to provide the contrast between that which is temporary and that which is permanent.

Disheveled, and in complete agony, we limped towards Eureka. Nothing was easy today, not even the last two miles. I closed my mind to the pain, and sprinted to the motel in town. I let my bike fall to the

70

ground in my hurry to register for a room.   But my friend Dave, where was he? A stranger behind me gave me the news.

"Your buddy is back on the highway. It looked like he needed help. After I register, I'll give you a lift."

Hearing this, the woman behind the counter, did one better.

"Here, take the keys to my truck. Go pick up your friend."

So I did. When Dave and I got to our room, he told me what happened.

"It was the mother of all blowouts. I thought the world had come to an end. Visions of nuclear holocaust ran through my mind. When I finally summoned the courage to open my eyes, I was relieved to see the earth still intact. The same could not be said about my rear tire. I've had flats before, but never one like this. Look at this tire, it has a hole in it the size of a quarter!

I nodded. In fairness to Dave, I wasn't listening that well. I was thinking. If I have to quit, what will my buddy do? Would he continue alone?

Using my arms, I pushed up out of the chair, wobbled out the door, and headed down the street for a bite to eat. It was past 11:00 p.m.

*　　　　　*　　　　　*

In the morning, I was pumping air in my tires in preparation for the fifty mile trip from Eureka to Whitefish when, Vrroommmm! Up pulls the largest Harley motorcycle I have ever seen. The rider, dressed in black leather, was a wild looking guy, with frizzy black hair, and a nasty mustache. I felt rather meek in my light gray tights standing next to my flimsy bicycle.

"Where you going," he demanded.

"North Carolina," I answered boldly. "Where are you headed?"

"A family reunion. I biked across country once. Had a great time. Went across Canada. Live up there. Came down here for the reunion."

My new friend talked in short, choppy, abrupt sentences. It was curious. Prior to this trip, I categorized people by dress, speech, or other unimportant traits. The bicycle and the highway are becoming great equalizers. This guy might be the one to toss me the keys to his Harley if I needed help.

"Looking forward to the family reunion. Love to play tug o' war. Have a good, safe trip. God bless you." With that, he roared off. God bless you from Mr. Harley. Wow.

In Eureka, I stopped at a drug store to pick up the anti-inflammatory medication and the ice pack that Dr. Bill suggested. For good measure, I also picked up an elastic knee brace. I have two hopes of continuing this trip—either the medication works or perhaps being out of the roller coaster hills will help. We will be in the plains in two more days.

Prior to leaving Eureka, Dave and I had phoned ahead for an appointment at the Glacier Cyclery in Whitefish for some needed repairs. We didn't quite make our 4:00 p.m. scheduled appointment. By the time we got to Whitefish, it was 5:30 p.m., a full thirty minutes past closing. Were they closed? No. Ron and Jan Brunk kept the shop open on a Saturday night, just to help us. They explained that it was over five hundred miles to the next bike shop, and they didn't want us to have any trouble. In appreciation, we bought several T-shirts and souvenirs.

Whitefish, twenty–five miles from Glacier, is one of several Montana towns that are being flooded with California celebrities. We can certainly see the allure of the area. Mountains circle the town, the old historic downtown buildings are in excellent condition, and it is just a few short miles to the spectacular Glacier National Park. We didn't see any celebrities though, and we stayed in the Super 8 Motel lobby for well over an hour.

*   *   *

"You get off your bike and take a picture of Mr. Bear!"

"But Dave, it is your camera. I doubt if I could use it."

On the road to Glacier National Park, Dave and I saw a small bear ambling across the highway. Tourists in their armored cars had stopped and were taking pictures of the beautiful animal. Attempting a different tack, I reminded Dave of how special these pictures might be.

As if to prove a point, Dave did indeed take the picture. On his bike. While racing by. With the armored cars in the way. Me? I kept Dave between me and the bear. No sense taking chances.

In a few miles, we arrived in the small resort village of Apgar, and Glacier National Park.

Priests, Mules, Indians and Iodex

"You are old," said the youth, "as I mentioned before
And have grown most uncommonly fat;
Yet you turned a back–somersault in at the door,
Pray, what is the reason of that?"

"In my youth," said the sage, as he shook his grey locks,
"I kept all my limbs very supple
By the use of this ointment—one shilling the box—
Allow me to sell you a couple."

—Lewis Carroll,
Alice's Adventures in Wonderland

"If Iodex saved the Jesuits, it will certainly do the job for you."

I had been complaining to the managers of the River Bend Motel, in Apgar, about the condition of my right knee. But they had the solution, and passed me a small bottle of Iodex.

I inspected it carefully. It had the texture of a vapor rub, and the coloring of molasses. It gave off a pungent aroma. Smelled sort of like an angry skunk dipped in road tar. The managers of the motel, Barbara and George, insisted on telling me more.

"Now, you won't find Iodex in many drug stores," Barbara explained. She appeared to be in her late fifties, with the look of a person that accepts hard work as a part of life. "It was developed about a hundred years ago, and is accepted in this part of the country as the best ointment for any type of pain or soreness." She said this with such great authority, how could I doubt her? Then too, George was nodding his head in the background. How could I dare question the healing power of this brownish gunk? I should sell this on the east coast, I was thinking. Perhaps I could set up the distribution outlets. I'll make a million dollars! As if I needed further proof, Barbara told me the story of the Jesuits.

"A few years ago, we were managing another motel in the area. It was the year of Montana's centennial, and many events were held to commemorate the milestone. George and I were busy that year, but not too busy to save the trip of the Jesuits.

"These two Jesuits decided, as part of the celebration, to reenact a missionary expedition that was made in 1889." She handed me a brochure on the Jesuits' trip. "Their route would take them over rugged terrain, and cover hundreds of miles. If they had planned properly, it would have been difficult enough. But the two Jesuits really hadn't spent enough time in preparation."

She lingered on the word "preparation." Somehow, I suspected this is where the Iodex was going to fit in.

"You see, they had come up with the idea of taking this trip only two months prior to their departure date. Neither one of them could ride a horse, or a mule for that matter.

"The day came for the Jesuits to start their great journey. We showed up out of curiosity—there were many other people there as well, including a television crew.

"The poor Jesuits had a rough start. One of them felt sorry for the mule, and he made the mistake of loosening the reins. The mule immediately took off, scattering the load everywhere. People were running in different directions, and the news crew was filming away."

Not a very promising start at all, I thought.

"Anyway, they finally took off on their journey. We followed their progress where we could, because they were such nice people." Barbara informed me that she and her husband are agnostics.

"As luck would have it, our paths did cross again. We were working a different motel, and learned that they were in the area. We went by to see them, and they were pleased to see us. Interest in their trip had kind of quieted, so I think they were glad for human company.

"They were both in excruciating pain. And that is how we saved their trip!" she exclaimed suddenly.

"Ma'am?" Either I was still giving the Jesuits' rough start proper consideration, and wasn't listening all that well, or I had just missed the point.

"Iodex," Barbara said impatiently. "We gave them the Iodex. They smeared it on their bodies, let it soak in overnight, and the next day they didn't have a single ache!"

"Oh, yes," I said. They were both eager for me to try the Iodex, so they loaned me the small bottle. Ricky will be glad to get this too, I thought.

Yes, Ricky! He has reappeared!

It was a joyous reunion. He had been alone for many days, and was grinning like a college freshman when we arrived in Apgar. It is apparent though, that he will not be able to complete the trip. His knee has not healed—it was by sheer determination that he made it to Glacier National Park.

Still, I now have a bottle of Iodex in my hands. Would it? Could it? Ricky and I smeared the gunk all over our legs, as Dave looked on in bemused silence.

Before turning out the light, I read, with great interest, the brochure the manager had given me on the Jesuits' trip.

Scholastic Luke Larson and Friar Pat Conroy did indeed ride nine hundred and eighty miles on horseback, dressed in black cassocks and wide-brimmed hats, as part of Montana's state centennial celebration in 1989. At the end of each day, the two men watered their horses and pack mules, and greeted tourists and visitors. The Blackrobes would tell them stories of how the early Jesuit missionaries lived and worked among Montana's native people.

"You never know what will spook a horse;" recalled Conroy, "big semi-trucks, bicycles, or culverts. Something whizzes past you and suddenly you're in a rodeo!"

The Christian mission work of one hundred years ago was part of an interesting period, not only in Montana, but in other areas of the country. One important organization, founded by Herbert Welsh, was the Indian Rights Association. It was founded on a twofold premise: one, that the Indians were capable of being civilized; and two, they had been thwarted in their attempts to become civilized by the injustices and inefficiencies of the federal government toward them.

The Indian Rights Association acknowledged the Christian motivations of its work. Welsh asserted that the Indian needed to be "taught to labor, to live in civilized ways, and to serve God." He remarked further that "the best Christian sentiment of the country is needed to redeem the Indian, to stimulate and guide the constantly changing functionaries of the government who are charged with the task of his civilization." So was the thinking of the period.

The journey took them a total of sixty-seven days. After taking a few days to rest, each returned to their full time apostolate.

There was no mention of Iodex.

*   *   *

Ricky and I woke up about the same time. We stared at each other, and then smiled. Had the Iodex worked? Were our knees suddenly cured? Have we discovered a miracle drug? No. We limped around the room; nothing had changed. We weren't too surprised.

I walked down to the hotel to check out. Barbara and George were both on duty, adding up receipts from the previous night. They grinned as I walked in the office.

"How's your knee?" they asked in unison.

"No better," I replied. "And my friend's knee is no better, either." I've never been one to mince words. But my friends didn't miss a beat.

"Very surprising," Barbara said. "But I bet you that your sore knee is caused by something other than cycling."

"Whaatttt?" was all I could manage.

"You bet," she continued confidently. "You have a potassium deficiency. You need to be taking supplements." She gave me a brochure on the subject. Coincidentally, she and George were distributors.

George warmed to the new topic. "These supplements should be an important part of your life. I've had friends that were sick, and in some cases dying, take the supplements and would you believe it, they immediately got better?" He moved in for the kill. "Now we're not supposed to make the claim that this will cure cancer, but do you know that I've had three friends that were dying of cancer take the supplement, and now they all have the disease in remission? You must admit it probably isn't a coincidence."

"Probably not," I noted. "I will certainly read up on this supplement issue. It just might be the key to saving the bike trip."

They were pleased to hear this. There is little doubt in my mind they will soon be telling other guests about the time potassium supplements saved the dreams of a crippled cyclist. The disappointing performance of the Iodex will be long forgotten.

"What do you have there, Bill?" asked Dave. He had been waiting, not so patiently, outside the office.

"Valuable information on potassium supplements," was all I could muster. He looked at me, I'm not sure he could tell I was kidding.

"Let's get outa here," he said, in a crabby tone of voice. He complained all morning about the smell of Iodex. I don't think he slept well.

*   *   *

With great reluctance, Dave and I got back on U.S 2, said good–bye to Ricky, and headed away from Glacier National Park. Much to our disappointment, we will not be able to cycle the Going–to–the–Sun Highway. Because of heavy, late season snows, the road is not open all the way through the park. We will need to detour south on US 2 around the base of the mountains, and enter the plains near the town of Browning.

As disappointing as this is, Dave and I consoled ourselves with one last look at Lake McDonald, and the magnificent mountains. I made a silent pledge to return—with or without my bike.

Struggling with tired legs, we targeted East Glacier as our destination. While the miles slowly clicked by, I thought some more of Ricky, and the people he met on his road to Glacier.

Tales from the Ultimate Camper

"Would you please tell, me, which way I ought to go from here?"
"That depends a good deal on where you want to get to," said the Cat.
"I don't much care where..." said Alice
"Then it doesn't matter which way you go," said the Cat.
"...so long as I get somewhere," added Alice as an explanation.
"Oh, you're sure to do that," said the Cat, "if you only walk long enough"

—Lewis Carroll,
Alice in Wonderland

For most of us, the transition from childhood to adult is a slow, painful, process. It is often a gradual accumulation of events that cause maturation. I don't think, for example, after a "first love," that boys automatically become men, or girls become women. Graduating from college does not automatically earn a young person the title of "adult," nor does being on your own, and paying your own bills. It is the collection of experiences—the successes and failures, the knowledge of right and wrong, and the understanding, and acknowledgment, that we all will do wrong—that gradually whittle away the innocence of youth.

As Ricky told us about his days on the road, I wondered how, just a year or two from now, he might view the odd collection of characters he encountered. Will he be more aware of the potential evil that could have existed in any one of these people? Will he realize that the people he met are "many in number" and that they represent the "other" part of America—the part that exists outside of carefully manicured subdivisions, and look–alike college campuses?

It is one thing to participate in carefully orchestrated events that create an awareness of life outside the familiar. Thanks to the excellent Christian examples of his parents, Ricky has done work for food banks, Habitat for Humanity, and many other charitable organizations. It is quite another matter, however, to be tossed into the ring, by yourself, without any directions or guidance. Ricky survived ten rounds on the road, but not without collecting a few cuts and suffering a couple of knockdowns. Over beers, on our last night together, Ricky told us about a few of the people he met.

"You guys scared me out of catching rides, so when I left Round Lake State Park, I decided to ride my bike as far as I could. I couldn't pedal uphill, because I couldn't push with my bad knee, so I'd walk up, and then get back on my bike and coast downhill. When the road was flat, I managed to pedal some, but that hurt too much. I did almost forty miles the first day, though, and made it to a campground near Clark Fork, Idaho.

"The next day, I made it to the corner of Highway 56 and 200. Usually, it doesn't bother me when I'm alone, but late in the second day, I really began to miss you guys. I also began to question myself. What am I doing out here all by myself, in this desolate area? I was hoping that the campground that was marked on my map would have a few fellow campers. In fact, it looked like it hadn't been used in years. Tall grass and scrubby weeds covered the area, and it was difficult avoiding the cans and bottles that littered the site.

"I didn't feel safe. I will never forget the loneliness of that quiet Montana night. Even the slightest noise scared me. Finally, after midnight, I fell asleep.

Dave and I shook our heads. Ricky continued.

"Shortly after 3:00 a.m., a loud roar woke me from my sleep. I couldn't figure out what the sound was, but it kept getting louder, and closer. Finally it came to me: it was a train! I became convinced I had pitched my tent on the tracks, so I grabbed as much as I could out of the tent, ran barefoot through the littered grounds, and for protection, I clung to a tree. Unknowingly, I had pitched my tent about three feet from the tracks. There was no sense going back to sleep after that, so I packed up all my things, and headed down Highway 56 in the dark."

This was the same highway that Dave and I had traveled. I had left Ricky a voice mail message, instructing him to stay with Alex and Eileen. These kind people, upon hearing of Ricky's plight, offered to take him in at no charge.

"Well, I never could figure out your messaging system," Ricky said, "so I didn't know about the Thompsons. I did find Bad Medicine campground, though. It was a beautiful, deserted place, but once again, there weren't any campers.

"By this time, I was running low on food, and I was down to my last Power Bar. Instead of eating that, though, I ate freeze–dried lasagna. Of course, you guys had the cooking gear, so I ate the lasagna dry. It was pretty gross."

Aarrgghh! As if to wash that thought out of our throats, we each took a swallow of beer. Ricky continued.

"I guess Bad Medicine campground was the low point. My knee had not improved at all. I knew you guys and my parents were worried about me, and I also realized that I would not be able to complete the trip. I didn't dwell on this too much, though, I had to get out of these backwoods, so I went back to hitchhiking. I soon got my first ride.

"Henry picked me up at a rest stop. He is sixty–nine years old, and has lived in Libby since 1922. He told me that the town is much worse now, since all the people from California, Washington, and Oregon have moved in, bought up the land, put up 'No Trespassing' signs, and brought the 'taxes, laws and cops' with them.

"Henry dropped me off in Libby and after pedaling part way through town, I stopped to talk to a fellow hitchhiker. He said, 'I don't know this area, but I know the country. Hell, nobody gives a damn if you want to camp somewhere. Pitch your tent any damn place you want. Just don't start a forest fire. All anybody does around here is get drunk and have fun. Everybody hates the cops and the cops hate them, so they get along just fine. The cops always go around trying to give those damn DWI tickets. Me, I get soaked by myself in the woods, and you want water? Most of the land is National Forest, and nobody can tell you not to camp there because everyone owns it.'

"This guy was loads of fun. After about fifteen minutes of his griping and rambling, I got back on my bike and hobbled to the edge of town. I stopped to phone my parents, but they weren't home. I was about to continue my struggles on the bike when a friendly couple walked up to ask me where I was headed.

"Maxine and Emil gave me a ride from Libby to Miller Creek. It was a short ride because they were going fishing. They dropped me off at Happy's Inn, where their friends Harvey and Delores keep shop. Laughing, Maxine said to Harvey, 'You ain't got a hair on your ass if you don't let Ricky take a free shower.'

"I couldn't believe my luck," said Ricky. "All these local people were helping me out. Harvey said he would have let me take a free shower even without Maxine's referral. I had showered and was packing my gear when Harvey introduced me to his friend, Don.

"Don was quite a character. He earns a living making cabinets and totem poles. He doesn't need much money, he told me, because he lives in a cabin powered by propane and a 12–volt battery. Claimed it was just like a regular house. 'I got a microwave, VCR and all,' he said.

'Car's all paid for, too. Got everything I need right here. Don't need the expense and pain of living in a big city.'

"Don kept me entertained with his stories as we drove towards MacGregor Lake. We passed through several miles of burned–out forests. All of the trees looked like toothpicks pointing towards the sky. Don fights forest fires, too. He told me he drove a CAT bulldozer right in front of the blazing fire.

"I had been wondering about the shattered back window of his station wagon. I asked Don to explain.

"'Yeah, that was bad,' he said. 'We were playing around with some armor piercing bullets—shooting at a big ol' iron rail out about a hunnerd yards away. My buddy says, 'Sheeiit, what was that that flew by?' Then I shoot again, and something else whizzed by my ear. We couldn't figger it out. Then I take another shot, and my window shattered. Then we got it—it was the damn ricochet! Scared the hell out of us!'

"I camped at MacGregor Lake where I met Jane and Diane. These two girls are both barmaids, and are heavily into the Montana drinking scene. They have old family roots—four generations—in the logging industry. But they are both moving away, trying to find places with younger populations and more active life. I enjoyed their stories—particularly the one about the bar where you skydive, then buy everyone a case of beer. Everyone drinks until the guys take their clothes off and swing naked from the chandeliers. Oh yeah, the girls get free shots for showing their breasts—shooters for hooters.

"I bought Jane and Diane ice cream. Then I met their neighbors, and their Uncle Bill, too. They sure knew a lot of people. Jane and Diane gave me a ride to Glacier National Park. You guys missed meeting them by about fifteen minutes."

Once again, Dave and I were amazed by Ricky's adventures.

"So what are you going to do now, Ricky?" Dave asked.

"Stay around here for a few days and do some exploring. Then I'll hitch a ride back to Whitefish, and from there, take a train back to Seattle. I'll stay with some relatives there for a while, and then fly back home.

"I don't regret anything that has happened to me on this trip. I've had more fun, and met more interesting people doing this than anything else I could have done. I'm already thinking of writing a book, or maybe some short stories about my experiences.

"Perhaps it's just as well that you guys continue this trip without me. You both are in a hurry to complete this trip by the first week in July, and I would just as soon stop and spend a few extra days in these interesting places. I'm not sure I could afford to travel in the style you guys are accustomed to, either."

I didn't offer any rebuttal to Ricky. Of course, Dave and I would prefer to take twelve weeks, not six, and kick around the backroads of the country. But Ricky will learn, when he too enters the doorway of middle age, that other demands and responsibilities have a way of imposing on personal desires. I only hope that when he is thirty–five, that his wife will be as understanding and as supportive as mine.

*   *   *

Our original destination for the evening was East Glacier. With our late start, however, we could not make our target. We were both wearing down, and it was an effort to pedal our loaded bikes. As we approached the small town of Essex, we noticed a billboard for the Izaak Walton Inn. We needed no further encouragement.

The Burlington Northern

What's the railroad to me?
I never go to see
Where it ends.
It fills a few hollows,
And makes banks for the swallows,
It sets the sand–a–blowing,
And the blackberries a–growing.

—Henry David Thoreau,
What's the Railroad to Me?

The Inn is reason enough to celebrate. It offers hearty meals, real beds, and hot showers. I have another reason to celebrate, however. The medication and ice packs are doing the trick. In just two days, my knee has shown great improvement, and as a result, I no longer dwell on quitting. I was giving Dave this good news, when something weird happened.

As if on cue, all of the diners suddenly left the restaurant. "Where's everybody going?" I asked Dave. Halfway through a medium rare steak, with all the trimmings, I was in no particular hurry to leave. But what if there was a fire? Or dancing girls? I was wasting my breath with Dave though; he had left the room with the others. I took one more bite, and joined them on the back porch.

I will be the first to admit it was a scenic spot. The Izaak Walton is, after all, "Surrounded by a million acres of wilderness." From the back porch there is a breathtaking view of the inspiring mountains. But why did everyone leave their dinner? My answer soon arrived.

It was the Burlington Northern Railroad. It is a tradition at the Izaak Walton Inn to stop whatever you are doing, and wave as the conductor, crew, and passengers of the train slowly roll by. It is a reciprocal arrangement—the train personnel were ready for us, too. In addition to waves, we received a friendly toot of the steam whistle. When the train disappeared, we all went back to the restaurant to finish our meal.

*   *   *

Dave and I have been following the northern tier of the Transamerican bicycle route. Our maps are developed and published by Adventure Cycling, which is a non–profit organization. The maps include such useful information as preferred routes for cyclists, hotel and campground locations, and colorful descriptions of the local history and geography.

Adventure Cycling promises that the Burlington Northern will be our faithful companion across northern Montana. Dave and I enjoyed reading about the history of this railroad, and the important part it played in the development of our western lands.

In the "Great Man" version of history, the story of these tracks is the story of James J. Hill, "the barbed–wire, shaggy–headed, one–eyed old sonofabitch of Western railroading," according to the Adventure Cycling narrative.

Hill's railroading began in the early 1870's, when he bought a bankrupt Minnesota railroad and turned it into a profitable carrier. This railroad transported wheat from the Red River Valley of North Dakota to Minneapolis, then carried finished goods back to the Red River farmers. Encouraged by this success, Hill turned his thoughts to completing a great railroad, one that would run all the way to the Washington coast.

With eight thousand men cutting through hillsides and filling in gullies, the railroad shot across the plains. With another six hundred and fifty men building bridges and laying tracks, the railroad made it from Minot to Havre, then from Havre southwest to Great Falls, all in a mere six months. By 1893, the line reached all the way to Puget Sound.

With the completion of the railroad, James J. had another problem. He needed people to live on the non–existent farms and in the non–existent towns along his railroad. Even the "major" towns of Havre and Great Falls were little more than a collection of tacky shacks.

James J. Hill financed a massive publicity campaign to attract people to live on the huge, empty grasslands, much of which Congress had deeded to Hill's railroad as an incentive to build the line.

"Land was sold for as low as $2.50 an acre with extravagant claims as to its fertility and productivity," writes historian Melvin Kazeck. The greater the distance from Montana and North Dakota, the more exaggerated were the claims for this New Eden. Hill's advertisements reached across the U.S., even to Europe.

Here's my favorite part.

"Low rates were established for the movement of household goods and farming equipment into the state; return rates on these same articles were so high that it was impossible for the farmer who had become discouraged to return to his native state," notes Kazeck.

The force of technology, however, was with the farmers. By 1900, modern agricultural tools were being mass produced. No longer was it a sideboard plow and a horse against the endless grasses of the plains. There were grain drills, discs, harrows, steel moldboard plows, steam-powered threshers, and new ideas about cooperative production.

New towns did indeed succeed. These towns were not, according to Montana historian K. Ross Toole, riotous places like the mining camps of the 19th century, or the oil towns of the early 20th century. Instead they were towns of utility. One street, one school, and one church. The grain elevator, the depot, and the bank.

"I don't know, buddy," I said to Dave as I finished my deep dish apple pie. "One grain elevator, depot and a bank? What about the motel? Where will we be staying?"

"They've had a few years to build a couple," Dave replied. "Maybe we'll get lucky."

*   *   *

The Burlington Northern thundered by several more times in the night. Dave and I stayed in our beds, though. There will be plenty of time for hospitality in the coming week.

At 10:00 a.m. we left the Izaak Walton Inn. On our first climb of the morning, we stopped and observed mountain goats casually enjoying a salt lick. A construction worker came over to talk to us.

"What? You guys are heading through Montana and North Dakota?" We nodded. "Well, you better enjoy the scenery while you can. There is nothing, but nothing, to look at for the next thousand miles!"

I'm sure he meant well, but he didn't exactly quell our fears about pedaling through the plains. The books and articles that Dave and I read prior to the trip all suggested that this part of the journey will be the most difficult.

Our destination for the evening is Shelby, Montana, approximately one hundred miles from Essex. First, though, we have to pedal through the "Indian" town of Browning.

Reservations about the Indians

"It is enough," he said. "Go, children of the Lenape, the anger of the Manito is not done. Why should Tamenund stay? The palefaces are masters of the earth, and the time of the Red Man has not yet come again. My day has been too long. In the morning I saw the sons of Unamis happy and strong; and yet, before the night has come, have I lived to see the last warrior of the wise race of the Mohicans."

—James Fenimore Cooper,
The Last of the Mohicans

Dave and I had been warned, several hundred miles back, about riding through Browning.

The advice we received was freely given. Dave and I didn't know enough to consider asking. To us, Browning was just another town on the map. We had planned to follow the Adventure Cycling route up through Canada, but the Going–to–the–Sun Highway was closed because of ice and snow.

"Don't look left, and don't look right;" one said, "wouldn't stop, either. Just get yourself through there."

Another offered, "I wouldn't stay there overnight. Be sure and travel through in the morning, or maybe early afternoon. When there's trouble, it's usually after dark."

Another person told this story: "Rumor has it a cyclist was shot and killed there a few years ago. He was in a Browning restaurant at noon, minding his own business, when a drunken Indian whirled around, fired a gun, and laid him out cold."

Even our conservative friend Alex flinched when we told him we might have to ride through Browning. "If I have to go to Browning, I usually go there early in the morning. I've never had any trouble, but I don't think they would bother with me."

If my guess is right, Alex probably rides into town with a loaded rifle in his pickup truck and a don't–mess–with–me" look in his eyes.

Dave doesn't have a gun, and I know, from experience, that my red hair and freckles aren't very intimidating.

Early on, I should have maturely handled my uneasy feelings about Browning. But I didn't. And now, staring down at the town of Browning, I opened my mouth to talk to Dave, but no words came out. Fear had shut down my vocal cords. Dave mistook my open mouth for a yawn.

"I don't believe you," Dave said, "for two hundred miles we've been talking about Browning. We might be about to die. And you're bored. Look at that place down there. Your Dad was right, we should have packed a gun. Close your mouth and let's map out a strategy."

I still couldn't speak.

Exasperated, Dave laid out the plan, "Let's stick together, Bill, ride as fast as we can, and get through this town."

"Yes," I croaked, and then looked at my watch. It was noon as we began our approach.

The outskirts of the city were not much different than many of the poorer areas back home. There were plenty of used car lots, cheap restaurants and mobile homes, but no McDonald's. I knew I was becoming paranoid, but where were all the McDonald's? Why wasn't there a McDonald's in Browning? Every civilized town has a McDonald's.

"Wait, Dave," I shouted. My old buddy was pulling away. Apparently he had forgotten about my knee injury. Intent, determined and oblivious, he continued to pedal at thirty miles per hour. Only at the first traffic light did I manage to catch him.

We cycled close to the center of town. Vandalized buildings with broken windows were the rule. The sidewalks were crowded with adults milling around as if they had no place to go. Children in ragged clothes played games in a vacant dirt lot. A lonely basketball goal leaned to the right as if searching for its missing rim.

Close to the center of town, we were unexpectedly joined by a couple of small Indian boys riding bicycles. They couldn't have been more than ten or eleven years old. Halfway down the city block, they challenged us to a race, and in the spirit of fun, we foolishly accepted. All four of us accelerated and raced recklessly down the narrow, crowded two–lane street.

"Stop! Stop!" I yelled at the children.

The light ahead of us had turned red.

"Watch out!" yelled Dave, "The light is red!"

Did they hear us?

In that split second, not knowing whether the boys would live or die, I remembered just a little of what I learned in college about Indian law. I have no rights on Indian land. United States laws do not apply here. There would be no investigation or trial. If those two boys get killed, Dave and I could very well be scalped and then burned at the stake. It would be an awful way to end the trip.

On the positive side, Dave and I might be famous, at least for a few days. Then again, maybe there would be a big cover-up, and no one would ever learn of our fateful ride. Perhaps the only clues to our trip would be scattered bike parts, and I suspect that these too would vanish in a hurry. A local entrepreneur would scoop up the parts, refurbish them, and advertise them in the newspaper.

Special sale! Gray tights! Aqua windbreaker! — $3.49.
Overloaded touring bike! Previously owned by engineer! — $29.95.

The boys didn't hear us. They plowed ahead, oblivious to our warnings, intent only on winning the race. At the last second, they turned their heads away from the light, back towards us, to make sure their lead was safe. Only then did they hear our warnings.

It was too late.

Through the busy intersection they raced, still laughing, as boys do, not realizing how quickly tragic accidents happen.

Dave and I stopped, got off our bikes, and prepared to run to the intersection.

I will never forget the sounds of the skidding tires. As if protected by Indian spirits, however, the boys miraculously weaved safely through the busy intersection, and laughing still, continued down the busy street.

They never looked back.

*   *   *

"They're just different," a stranger told us.

We were talking to a couple of older gentleman outside a grocery store in Cut Bank. The town of Browning was now thirty–five miles behind us. He continued.

"For the most part, we don't have that many problems. But from time to time, there are confrontations. Most of the trouble comes at the end of the month. They get checks from the government, just for being Indians, so they have little incentive for work. As soon as they get the money, some of them buy all the booze and drugs they can get and go on their sprees.

"The government provides housing for these people, too. The day after some units were recently completed, the plumbing was ripped out, sold, and the money used to purchase more drugs."

The other gentleman offered his view.

"The federal government has spent an incredible amount of money helping the Indians. Those dollars bought better education, health care, housing, public employment, and roads. But you know what? You can't throw money at this problem and expect it to be fixed. See, unless these dollars are used to build factories, or start farms, you haven't got anything. All the money we throw at them now goes right towards feeding a welfare dependence."

Prior to the trip, Dave and I were blissfully ignorant about the many issues of the American Indians. Certainly it is not a topic that often comes up in Los Angeles. In South Carolina, the concern is with the plight of blacks, not Indians. I once made a trip to Cherokee, North Carolina, however, and saw the descendants of a once great and proud race selling cheap trinkets, and posing in front of tepees. In fact, the Cherokee never lived in tepees; they lived in stable communities with huts and cabins. I've never gone back to Cherokee. It saddens me to see trinkets and souls being sold at the same time. Like many, I find it easier to sweep unpleasant issues under the carpet.

"Dave, I'm embarrassed about the way I felt going into Browning. I let unsubstantiated rumors affect my thinking. So many times, I've seen the same thing happen down south. Whites will easily accept the stereotypes of blacks and, I'm sure, the reverse is true. I always like to think I know better, but today, my behavior was no better.

"My parents always told me to be fair to people and today I forgot their lesson. I'm sure many Indians hate and resent white people. Can you blame them? After all, this was their land only two hundred years ago. Now the only land they have is the reservation. I remember my history. The reservations are on land that no one else wanted."

"That's true," Dave replied, "but that was a hundred years ago. What excuse does the current generation have?"

Down & Out
in Chester, Montana

"The doors of heaven and hell are adjacent and identical."

—Nikos Kazantzakis,
The Last Temptation of Christ

Leaving Browning was no more difficult than dropping off a bad date. Once through with the ordeal, there is no great desire to review the unpleasantness. Only time can heal the pain. If you are lucky, the event will take on a different light and perhaps be re–told in a year or two with an ironic grin, or a rueful grimace.

As Dave and I distanced ourselves from this troubled town, I looked over my shoulder—not at Browning, but at the receding beauty of the northern Rockies. Each rotation of the pedals takes us further from the snowy peaks, the splashing streams and waterfalls, and into the treeless rolling hills of the northern high plains.

I will miss the far west. It is the part of the country I thought of most during the endless hours of training. Many times, high expectations lead to disappointment. Not this time. I will never forget the beauty of the area or the quality of the people. This was the good date. This was the date that leaves you wanting more. With little expectation that good times were ahead, I took one last look at the Rockies, and headed towards the town of Shelby.

*   *   *

Despite its huge size, less than one million people live in Montana. Farming and ranching are the predominant industries. Small support towns greet us from time to time, usually with no more than a three–aisle grocery store, a cafe, and a couple of bars. Perhaps the bars were doing the majority of the business. Along the highways in Montana are small white crosses, marking the places where people have lost their lives in car accidents. There are a lot of small white crosses.

Although we had expected dry and dusty conditions, the endless farmland seems well–watered and thriving. Still, when Dave and I stop at the small cafes, the farmers and ranchers are all discussing the weather.

"I hear Joe got rain over at his place last night."

"Well, I wish it would come over this way, we sure could use it."

Heads nod in silent agreement. More coffee is poured, and the conversation continues. We feel as out of place as a "No Smoking" sign in these small cafes. We don't belong in their club, but we usually receive polite nods and hellos.

To our surprise and chagrin, the plains are not as flat as we expected. Long, rolling hills make the cycling a constant challenge. Visualize one–hundred tea cups lined rim to rim. Down the side of the cup, pedal in the trough, climb up the other side, only to face the next cup. This was the highway from Browning to Shelby.

"We only have seven more days of these cups if we average ninety miles a day." I gave Dave this information as we fixed my first flat of the day, a block from the motel where we had spent the night in Shelby. Dave looked at me like I was nuts. We cycled one hundred and two miles yesterday, and Havre, a hundred miles away, was our destination for today.

The first hour was relatively easy. The rain eased, and we averaged thirteen to fourteen miles per hour, which is our normal speed with loaded bikes. We stopped for our first break at 10:00 a.m. at a small "mom and pop" bar and cafe. In many ways, this cafe reflects life in rural Montana.

The building had seen better days, but I'm not sure when. It presented a tired, worn and weather–beaten appearance, as if fatigued from the battle with the elements. Located, quite simply, in the "middle of nowhere," there was not even a tree to keep the faded brown building company. We pedaled through the mud and gravel parking lot, and placed our bikes against the outside wall.

The interior was much the same. Nothing fancy here. No hanging ferns or glass–topped tables at this stop. The husband and wife team who own and run the bar are also typical of the people we have met in Montana. They seem a lonely lot initially; not likely to initiate conversation.

After a few questions, though, you may discover a very warm and friendly side. Weather is a great ice breaker in these parts.

"How's business today?" I inquired.

"Slow."

"Did you get much rain last night?"

"A little."

"My friend and I got caught in a downpour this morning when we left Shelby."

"Shelby? Why, that's where my nephew lives. He's got a farm up there. Grows a lot of wheat. Been there some fifteen years now. Don't really see much of him, though. Stays pretty busy, I guess. Say, where did you all say you were headed?"

Once she got started, it was as though we were old friends.

We paid for our Snickers bars and headed out.

*　　　　*　　　　*

Like a jilted lover, the Rockies tried to pull us back west. Howling easterly winds ripped at our faces, clawed at our bodies, and flattened our spirits.

The winds were blowing at least thirty miles per hour, and slowed our speed to that of a old woman on a slow walk. Every ounce of energy was used to preserve this lowly pace. Dave and I stood up while pedaling in an attempt to gain additional leverage, but that didn't work either. Turn a hair dryer on to "high," place it next to your ear, and at the same time, run in place for three hours. That's what it was like.

At 2:00 p.m., we pulled into the small crossroads town of Chester, and entered the local cafe. The relief from the torture was immediate. We lounged for close to an hour, sipping on hot tea, and talking about our next step. Should we stop, or should we continue to fight the wind?

The answer appeared in the form of the MX Motel, a small establishment with about fifteen rooms. We didn't ask, but it is our guess that the cheerful, efficient, woman who checked us in is the owner, manager, and cleaning crew. When I inquired about ice for my swollen knee, this kind lady walked over to the supermarket, bought the ice, and delivered it to our room. Between the Motrin and the ice packs, my knee continues to improve.

For the first time during the trip, Dave and I took an afternoon nap. What a pleasure! After two weeks on the road, we enjoyed the luxury of a free afternoon. Meanwhile, the wind and rain continued to beat against the door of our room.

I am ashamed to admit it, but I have developed hysterical tendencies. I was convinced, for example, that I would not survive the federal campground. In Eureka, I thought my sore knee might mean the end of the trip. I am now convinced that we will never leave the state of Montana. During my afternoon nap, these miserable thoughts wouldn't leave me alone. I dreamt I was at an Eagles concert, and the band got stuck on the same lyric from "Hotel California." First, the words were delivered to the audience and then they forgot the masses and shouted and pointed at me:

"You can check out any time you want, but you can never leave."

*   *   *

We walked across the street for dinner. In spite of the afternoon nap, I was not in a cheerful frame of mind. I always try to maintain a positive attitude, yet here I was, a grown man, crying about the wind.

"Dave, if these winds keep up, we'll never get out of these plains. We won't get home until September. We'll be lucky to get to North Carolina before it snows!"

"Bill, you need a drink!"

He was right, of course. After the second scotch, my perspective began to lighten and the discussion turned towards luck and life.

"Bill, do you get the feeling someone is looking out for us? We could have been blown off the road today, or worse, the headwinds might have picked up yesterday, and forced us to spend the night in Browning. Remember the 'Corridor Effect?' I think doors are sometimes opened in ways we can never predict."

"Uh–huh," I mumbled.

"Poor Ricky. I sure hated to leave him behind, but he really seemed to be taking it all in stride. In spite of his misfortune, he was intent on having his own adventure. And the people he met. What an unlikely bunch, but they mostly tried to help him out. I believe this has everything to do with his attitude. How many of these folks would have offered their assistance had Ricky been rude, acted smart or indignant?"

"Uh–huh," I mumbled.

Dave continued, "I remember our high school football coach used to say, 'Luck is when preparation meets with opportunity.' Funny, he always said this during practice—the preparation—and before the game—the opportunity. You know what? He was right."

*　　　　　*　　　　　*

After dinner, we went back to the motel and, for the first time, got out the map of the United States. Even though we feel good about how far we have come, it is frightening to see how far we have to go. Using the Adventure Cycling mileage, we figure that to finish in New Bern, North Carolina by July 4th, we need to average ninety–four miles a day. This seems impossible, since we have experienced some pretty gruesome days—like today—without even coming close to that average.

*　　　　　*　　　　　*

When we awoke, we listened, first for the wind, and then the rain. After yesterday's beating, we have learned that the former, not the latter, is the cyclists greatest enemy. We listened attentively—all was quiet. When we opened the door, we found that the wind had shifted and the rain had stopped. Perhaps we will make it out of Montana.

While the gods were still smiling, we hurriedly packed our gear and left the town of Chester. What a difference twenty–four hours can make. A cautious tailwind now caressed our backs, and only a light drizzle reminded us of our nightmarish day.

It was a beautiful day to cycle. We set a blistering eighteen mile per hour pace as we raced through the towns of Inverness, Joplin, and Kremlin. The light wind seemed to fairly lift us over the rolling hills. We lunched in Havre, and at 3:00 p.m., had set our sights on Harlem, which is over one hundred miles from Chester.

A Woman who Never Forgot

Nothing but the dead and dying in my little town.

—Paul Simon,
My Little Town

As a last resort, I left Dave by the side of the highway, and rode solo to Harlem, a distance of about ten miles. Dave couldn't go any further because of two broken spokes on his rear tire. Ordinarily, these are easily fixed, but the lug on his freewheel was so tight he was unable to loosen it to perform the repairs. I told Dave not to worry, that I would check into the motel— our maps indicated that there was one in Harlem—and I would soon be back with help. It turned out to be a lie.

The motel in Harlem was closed, and from appearances, it had been for years. Carefully, I circled the deserted parking lot—avoiding large shards of glass—hoping that if I circled enough, it might magically re-open. A weathered "For Sale" sign was tacked to the side of the dirty white brick building. The sign was tacked at an odd angle, giving me the impression that the owner had put it up as an afterthought, thinking that while nobody of sound mind would buy the place, it was worth the investment of a nail and a sign, just in case a bigger fool happened by.

I left the motel, and rode through town. Several times I slowed to talk with people, but they ignored me, as if I was carrying news of a tax increase. In vain, I searched for an open shop, or helpful people, but found neither. There seemed to be no other choice than to go back and give Dave the bad news. I sat down near a stop sign on the outskirts of town to consider my options when a pickup truck pulled over.

"Was that your friend back there on the highway?" In the truck was a man, his wife, and two children.

"Yes," I said.

"We almost asked him if he needed some help, but we figured he was tired of biking and just wanted to walk for a while."

"Uh, no," I responded. This was no time be bashful.

"I don't know you, but the biggest favor you could do for me would be to go back and pick him up. It would really help."

The man didn't hesitate. He gave me a big smile, and said they would be back. In a few minutes, they returned with Dave.

"Where are you all staying tonight?" the man asked.

I confessed that I had no idea. Dave's smile faded as he realized there was no motel, no campground, and certainly no bike shop to fix his broken spokes.

"Well you could stay with us, but we live forty miles up the road on the Canadian border. You probably don't want to go that far out of your way. Why don't you throw your bike in the back, and we'll drive around town. Maybe I can help you find a place to stay."

He had no more luck than we did. As a last resort, I asked him to stop at the police station. Maybe they could help, I reasoned.

Two women in their seventies were working behind the counter. In contrast to the town, it was a neat, clean building. I did the talking.

"Ma'am, we were wondering if you could recommend a place for us to stay tonight. We are biking across the country, and need a place to sleep."

The first woman thought for a minute, and told us we could camp in a vacant lot next to the police station. It took me all of two seconds to realize I wouldn't feel safe even doing that.

"Thank you ma'am. I tell you, though, we have a lot of expensive equipment. I would really feel better sleeping in the jail! Could we do that?" I asked hopefully. At that time, the second woman spoke up.

"How would you boys like to camp in my backyard? I'll even throw in a hot shower." It didn't take us long to whip out the "yes ma'am's" and "thank you ma'am's." We followed Liz Parenteau, a member of the Harlem City Council, to her home.

"I grew up in Harlem," she said in response to my question. "It was a prosperous town then. There were more farms, employing more workers. Automation and productivity had not yet altered the landscape. Did you see any deer or antelope riding into Harlem?"

"Yes," I said.

"If you boys had been on the same road fifty years ago," she said, "you wouldn't have seen any animals. With fewer farms these days and fewer people, the animals are becoming more abundant."

We were talking on the back porch of her modest, well-kept home. Dave and I had already pitched our tent in her backyard, taking care to keep out the mosquitoes. My buddy was attempting to fix his spokes, and even with the benefit of some wrenches, was not having any luck. As darkness moved in, the mosquitoes became even more aggressive. What was this woman doing here?

While married, Liz lived in the Seattle area, and a few of her family members still live in the Pacific Northwest. I mentally compared the beauty of Washington state, with what I have seen in Harlem. No, it doesn't make any sense.

Dave wasn't making any progress with his bike until Liz mentioned that her neighbor was a mechanic. Amazingly, when we went next door, her friend had an air wrench which loosened the freewheel. Dave soon fixed his spokes, and when he finished, we all moved inside. She told us more about Harlem.

"I'm not blind to the problems that we face. Many factors contributed to our decline—problems such as unemployment brought on by farm automation, and the difficult Indian issues. Many people think the relocation of U.S. 2 is the only reason we are having problems. No longer do traveling motorists pass through the business center of town. Sure, it's had an effect, but it's not the only reason we are struggling.

"The town needs leadership. There is an attitude these days of, 'It's not my problem', and many people say, 'Don't bother me, I've got enough troubles of my own.' Harlem needs people that want the town to survive. Take that motel you found closed. It's important that we have a motel, and I have tried to find ways to open it again. I am only one person, however, and we need others to stay and fight for improvements.

"I've thought about this a lot. At my age, it is tempting to sit in a rocker and talk about the way things used to be. That's not the road I'll be taking. I'm even thinking of running for mayor in the next election."

I asked my question, even though I knew the answer, "Why did you move back to Harlem, Liz?"

"It's my home, fellows." she replied. "My heart and soul are in this town."

*   *   *

It was close to 11:00 p.m. and time to get some sleep. Distant thunder rumbled in the background. Nothing new here. Every time we camp, it rains. Liz told us that we could come inside and use one of her extra bedrooms if it rained, but we nodded politely and told her that we had no intention of imposing any further.

We should have imposed. In short order, Dave and I were in danger of drowning in our tent. For some perverse reason, we ignored Liz's pleas to come inside. What were we thinking about? Thunder and lightening exploded right over our tent, and the storm raged on for most of the night. Finally, just before dawn, the storm passed. We got up early, packed our gear, and went in to have coffee with Liz. After our first cup, we asked her how we could thank her. "Oh, you could take me into town for breakfast," she said shyly. So we did. The cafe she selected was in the middle of town, and judging from the number of people who said "hello" as we walked by, she is, indeed, well known in the community.

"I'd like to prove to a few of the town folk that it's possible to take in an occasional stranger without worry." Liz said, after a bite of her scrambled eggs. "We're a small town, and I'm sure that by 8:00 p.m. last night, everyone knew that you were staying with me. I bet most of the people thought that you would turn out to be robbers, or worse. Well, they're wrong, and I'm getting a free breakfast out of it!"

After our meal, it was time to leave Harlem and Liz Parenteau. She had given us much to consider.

*   *   *

"You guys have a long way to go!"

We were talking to two touring cyclists that were headed in the opposite direction. Virginia was their starting point—in a few weeks they plan to be in Washington state.

It is difficult to comprehend. We have passed the eleven hundred mile point, and are feeling proud of our accomplishments. Yet, they are right. We are not even one-third of the way through our journey.

We lunched at a small town, Malta, which advertises itself as the "home of the friendliest people." I never believe signs like this. I was prepared to be ignored, spat upon, or pounded by passing thugs, but three people stopped me to ask if I needed help with directions.

Here's to Malta, home of the friendliest people!

Father Ralph

"For now we see through a glass, darkly;
but then face to face: now I know in part;
but then shall I know even as also I am known."

I Corinthians 13:12

"Bill, is that you?"

I peered through the cigarette smoke in the bar and tried to see who was calling me. It certainly wasn't Dave. I left him back up on what used to be U.S. 2. The highway was under construction, and as a result, we were forced to ride on a mixture of gravel and dirt.

On this hot day, Dave punctured a tire five miles from Saco—our destination for the night—and for reasons known only to Dave, he hauled his bike into a swamp to repair the flat. He waved me on when I rolled by, I think he knew that I wasn't going to stop and help him under those conditions. Saco is known as the mosquito capital of the western hemisphere—they are as big as buzzards and meaner than mashed cats. So I waved at Dave, screamed, "good luck, buddy," and dutifully pedaled into Saco, which is the boyhood home of famed broadcaster, Chet Huntley.

There was good news and bad news in Saco. The good news was that there was a motel. The bad news was the motel. There was no office attached to these units—check–in was at the bar. And no, don't bother showing your credit card, only cash is recognized in this lonely outpost. But who was that calling my name?

As I peered through the cigarette smoke, my worst fears were confirmed. It was that priest—the same priest that refused to accept my confession on the plane trip to Bellingham. How could I ever forget that deeper–than–sin voice that thinly masks the razor sharp insight of a crack detective?

Father Ralph, as he calls himself, is in his mid–forties, with the frame and countenance of someone accustomed to respect. Not that he is overtly threatening—in fact, I suspect most people are so charmed by his wide–eyed innocence and laughing eyes that they completely miss the point that this is a dangerous man. Anyone that wants to peer into your soul should be treated with the utmost caution.

"How has your trip been so far, Mr. Bill?"

"Fine, Father Ralph. Dave and I have had a great time. We have been exposed to the plight of the Indians, and have also gotten a feel for the loneliness of the land out in the plains." I tossed Father Ralph a few other bones, hoping that he would gnaw on the stories and leave me alone. Not Father Ralph—he requires more than an executive overview.

"Mr. Bill, one of the reasons for this trip was for you to find your lost soul. Have you had any luck?" Father Ralph took a long swig of beer.

"No, Father Ralph, I haven't. I think finding my soul is going to be more difficult than I imagined. I think I have, however, gotten a feeling for the soul of this part of the country. The Indian issues seem to overshadow most other concerns. An incident earlier today, near the town of Glasgow, reminded me of the constant tension.

"I was sitting in front of a small convenience store. Dave was a few miles further back on the highway fixing a flat. I took the opportunity to stretch and slowly drink a large orange Gatorade. An old pickup truck pulled into the parking area, and three male occupants, all in their early twenties, got out and started inside. They were of Indian ancestry.

"'How are you guys doing?' I asked.

"'Fine,' said one, 'We've been water skiing on the lake.'

"'Beautiful day for that,' I responded. 'You headed back out there?'

"'Yup. It's located on the Fort Peck Indian Reservation. Do you want to go with us?'

"This friendly invitation, Father Ralph, contained a challenge. It was delivered with an emphasis on the words 'Indian Reservation.' In addition, the three stared at me rather intently.

"'I'd love to,' I answered. 'But I can't today. I need to be in New Bern, North Carolina by July 4th. Do you guys know a shortcut?'

"That broke the ice. They laughed, asked a few questions about our trip, and went in the store. I must confess to a small amount of relief.

"The daily struggles most people endure just to eke out a living has also made an impression on me. While I worry about finding my soul, these people are worried about paying their bills. I've always given thanks for the material things I have, but these last two weeks I realize how fortunate I really am."

Father Ralph nodded his head. And nodded his head some more. Feeling somewhat nervous, I continued.

"But you know what has surprised me the most? It is the number of people that want to do the same thing that Dave and I are now doing. It seems to us that many people are in search of their soul, that many people want to get away from the tedium of everyday existence. It doesn't matter what race of people, they could be white, black, or red, many have approached us and finished up a conversation by saying 'Boy, I sure wish I could do what you guys are doing.'

The priest smiled ever so slightly at this news. Perhaps he was thinking that the more people searching for their souls would translate into increased church attendance, and bigger offerings.

Out of the corner of my eye, I saw Dave racing into beautiful downtown Saco, which with its dirt streets from the construction, looked like a scene from "Rawhide." Dave, with his intent, angry expression looked like that coyote character in the Roadrunner cartoons. I caught Dave's attention, and motioned him to come into the bar to drink a beer or two before dinner. When I turned back to Father Ralph, he was gone—only a half empty beer bottle and a generous tip were left on the table.

*   *   *

Dave was in no mood for frivolities. Looking kind of lumpy from his brief, intense, exposure to the mosquitoes, he had no patience for listening to my story about Father Ralph. Knowing how these bad days can be—having had two or three myself—I waved the bartender over and ordered up a couple more cold beers.

It was prom night in Saco, and the bar closed early. In the diner next door, we feasted on steak and potatoes covered in gravy. We had some trouble distinguishing the steak from the potato, but considering our fortunes of the past two days, we had no right to complain.

"By the way, Dave, what were you doing in that ditch back there?" I ventured.

"Well, it seemed like a good idea at the time," he said. "While removing my rear wheel, however, I got hit with gravel from passing cars.

"By the way, why was the entire highway being repaired at once? Couldn't they do it in sections? No, they had to do they whole damn thing at once. It may be easy on the construction crew, but it makes for hellish riding on a bicycle.

"I'm sure that flat was caused by riding on the gravel. I was really worried about breaking another spoke. The dust and gravel from passing cars was so bad, I decided to pick up the bike and carry it off the road to fix the flat. Big Mistake! I didn't realize the road ran right along side a swamp. The mosquitoes were on me like fleas on a dog. I had been severely bitten all over, and was heavily into chemical warfare, when I realized that this was a lost battle. That's when you arrived. I waved you on since there was no point in both of us getting eaten alive! I finally wised up and moved the bike back up on the highway and fixed the flat. Then I sprinted into Saco in a crazed fit of fear induced adrenaline mixed with anger at the Montana State Highway Commissioner and myself for being in Saco, Montana instead of on a sailboat in the Virgin Islands."

Dave was wound up again.

"When I finally pulled into town, I was completely exhausted. I had burned up every ounce of energy I had trying to get through the seven miles of road construction quickly and alive. I looked around and there you were standing on the street corner holding out a cold beer. I can't recall having ever seen a more welcome sight."

Upon hearing this, I began to wonder about Father Ralph. Wasn't I in the bar when Dave pulled in? Wasn't Father Ralph in the bar? Am I losing my mind?

A Solitary Cyclist

O who will walk a mile with me
Along life's merry way?
A comrade blithe and full of glee,
Who dares to laugh out loud and free,

And let his frolic play,
Like a happy child, through the flowers gay
That fill the field and fringe the way
Where he walks a mile with me.

—Henry Van Dyke

Dave and I believed, prior to departing for the trip, that we would meet a number of fellow cyclists. Naturally, they would all look like us, dress like us, be our age, and have the same goals. We never considered that there would be cyclists that might be different from us.

Husband and wife cycling across the country on their honeymoon? A long shot. With her sister? Not a chance.

A successful, fifty–five year old man riding his bike across the country, all by himself? Not likely, yet here we were having dinner with Alex. He was in a gregarious mood. I think he was delighted to find understanding company for the evening.

When I studied Alex, it occurred to me that I could be him in twenty years. Both of us are tall and thin with lean frames, but more than that, we both have something of an independent spirit. Alex, too, had left his wife and family behind upon hearing the call of the open road.

"No, this is not the first trip I've taken by myself," Alex said in response to Dave's question. "I've taken many tours across the country before, and have also toured in Europe and Africa. On this trip, I plan to cycle to Nova Scotia. I'm fortunate. I've been very successful in my career, and as a result, now have the time and money to indulge myself with these trips."

"You must get lonely traveling by yourself," I replied. Cycling is a lonely sport, but to be completely by yourself would be very difficult.

"It is tough," Alex said, "usually I travel with my partner, but he wasn't able to make this trip. Still, I often run into people like you, that understand what it's like out on the road. At my age, it is difficult finding a compatible riding partner. Plus, you can really meet some strange people out here on the road, you know."

Dave and I laughed, and then my old buddy explained the curious couple we had met earlier in the day.

"About an hour after breakfast, we were drinking Gatorade outside a convenience store, when a single cyclist crested a small hill and coasted into the parking lot. It was a woman cyclist! Bill and I glanced at each other in surprise.

"She wasn't alone, though. A few minutes later, her partner crested the hill and joined us outside the store. He was wearing a Hard Rock Cafe T-shirt.

"This was their breakfast stop. The woman, Kathy, went inside and came out with a half-dozen granola bars. While she was inside, we learned from her friend, Bob, that they had started in Seattle the day after us, and planned to finish in Maine. Kathy was kind enough to offer us a granola bar, but we didn't accept. Bill explained that we had just eaten a large breakfast of omelets and pancakes. With this news, Bob glared at Kathy.

"During the day, we passed each other several times. The last time was late in the afternoon, just after we crossed into North Dakota. They had stopped on the shoulder of the highway, to fix a flat tire.

"'Pump harder! Pump harder!'

"Kathy was screaming at Bob as he fixed her flat.

"'You're not doing it right,' she said. 'Pump harder! Pump harder!'

"It was not a pleasant sight. Bob was on his knees, sweating like a pig, trying to inflate her flat tire. Every few seconds, she looked at her pressure gauge, and repeated the same order.

"'Pump harder! Pump harder!'

"I felt sorry for the guy, so I told them we'd buy the beer at the hotel in town. Bob got very sullen and quiet, and didn't say anything. By now we figured that old Bob didn't have much say in things.

"'Absolutely not,' she said, 'we prefer to camp.'

"I don't think she was speaking for Bob. From his sad, pained expression, I suspect he would have loved a cold beer.

"Bob had yet to say a word," Dave continued. "It was obvious to me he was completely dominated by this Amazon. I'm not sure he wanted to be on this trip. It certainly didn't look like he had done much training. Or if he had, it was done mostly in the bowling alley. She, on the other hand, had muscles that would intimidate any man. I wouldn't want to mess with her."

"Me either," Alex said, "she sounds like trouble. It reminds me of something that once happened to me." He took another sip of wine and asked, "Have you ever been on a trip where you really didn't get along with the people you were with?"

"Oh, yes," we said.

He continued, "A friend of mine and I used to cycle together quite a bit. We were planning our next trip, when we decided to invite some more people. Neither of us had friends that liked to cycle, so we reviewed some of the "partner wanted" ads in the cycling magazines."

I knew the ads that Alex was discussing. Many individuals, both male and female, place these ads in the bicycling magazines. Often accompanying the ads are brief descriptions of the proposed trip, and perhaps one or two personal notes.

> Wanted: Male or Female to share exp. of a lifetime on transcontinental bike trip. Plan to finish in 6 wks on west to east rte. leaving in mid–May. I am a carefree, happy, go-lucky, single white male looking for my life–mate. Call Georgie, 1–900 GET–REAL.

Alex continued. "We finally found a couple of guys that were planning the same type of trip that we were considering. We decided it would be fun to travel together.

"My friend and I like to take our time on a tour. We were particularly looking forward to this trip, because neither one of us had ever pedaled through the southwest. We planned to ride fifty to seventy–five miles a day, but if something struck our fancy, we wanted to stop for a few days and explore. It turned out our new partners didn't have the same schedule.

"It was a disaster from the start. We didn't really get along, and we were constantly arguing about where to stop, or what route to take. It certainly wasn't working out.

"Finally, in Arizona, our opportunity came. We agreed to make a right hand turn on a particular road. Our two 'guests' missed the turn, and continued to the east. I caught up with my buddy, and we watched them as they cycled away. Here was our opportunity to get rid of these clowns. We did have one problem, though. We were carrying some of their gear, and they had some of ours. What would you have done?"

I laughed, "That's easy. I would have changed my name, painted my bike, and headed the other way. But what did you do, Alex?"

"We decided to catch up with them. Guess where they were?"

We had no idea.

"At a McDonald's." He fairly sneered when he said this. In his mind, that summed up the whole experience.

"Another time," he said, "my wife and I took a trip together. I spent a lot of time finding just the right trip for the two of us. I finally arranged a combination bed and breakfast and cycling trip."

We could hear just a hint of sarcasm creep into his voice.

"The first day we rode six miles," he said, "the next day we rested."

He took a swallow of his wine. I don't think he enjoyed that trip.

We never did see Alex again. He told us he was an early riser, but still, since we were travelling the same route, we expected that we might catch him during the day.

Maybe he doesn't cycle with strangers anymore.

No Charge for the Fruit

Through this toilsome world, alas!
Once and only once I pass;
If a kindness I may show,
If a good deed I may do
To a suffering fellow man,
Let me do it while I can.

—Unknown

From Williston to Parshall, North Dakota, we cycled in an area that Adventure Cycling calls "mild badlands." For a seventy–mile stretch, in searing heat, there was not a restaurant, store, or service area. Even though we had topped off all our water bottles prior to leaving Williston, we were running on empty for the last few miles before New Town. From there, it was an hour before we reached a small motel in Parshall. A middle-aged woman, and her son, in his thirties, were sitting outside enjoying the warm breezy evening. We told them of our struggles.

"At least you made it," she said. "I've heard a few accounts of cyclists who didn't make it. They run out of water, come close to heat exhaustion, and have to sit by the road and wait to be picked up."

Dave and I have learned not to be in any particular hurry when we arrive in a small town. It's a pleasant change from the jobs we left back home. There you are expected to show up with an objective, get the information you need, and move on to other matters. Here, along the lonely roads of the high plains, things are different. We sit down, talk, and listen to the local concerns.

Parshall, a couple of miles off the main highway, is located on an Indian Reservation. Approximately fifteen hundred people live here, with half being of Indian descent. It is evident to us that this small town has a considerable amount of civic pride. The streets are clean, and the shop windows and homes are well kept. If a town could talk, Parshall would whisper, "I'm trying."

The woman is the manager of the motel, and it is her son that is visiting. In addition to this job, she also works at the bank in town. I followed her into the office to register.

107

"Is the grocery store still open?" I asked. Dave and I have lately added apples and peaches to our diet.

"No, it isn't. We do have a grocery store, but it closes at 6:00 p.m. It opens back up early in the morning," she responded. "I don't know how fresh the fruit will be, though. In this part of the country we don't always get good fruit."

I thanked her for the information, picked up the key, and headed to our room.

The room is as neat and tidy as the town. It offers all of the standard amenities—two large comfortable beds, color cable TV, a desk, a steaming hot shower, and extra homey touches such as a quilted bedspread and matching curtains. Dave and I took our showers and headed out the door for dinner.

I don't know why I was surprised. A generous basket of fruit and a large pitcher of iced tea had been placed on the picnic table for our enjoyment. It came out of her refrigerator—there was no charge. She thought it would make us feel better. We sat down and enjoyed our fruit as she talked about Parshall.

"In many ways, the issues facing our town are probably the same as those facing the other small towns that you fellows have passed," she said. "Improved productivity in farming comes at the expense of jobs for farm workers. There just aren't as many jobs as there used to be."

I was taught in college that this is one of the laws of capitalism. Productivity gains are necessary to compete in the global marketplace. Away from an academic setting, the law now seems a bit harsh. Briefly, I thought of my college professor that taught urban geography. He was paid big dollars by my alma mater to form statistical conclusions about towns such as Parshall. Perhaps he would choose Parshall as one of the cities doomed to die.

She continued, "The young people all migrate to the larger cities. It is difficult to survive with this displacement of energy and vitality. I enjoy living here, but what does Parshall hold for the young people?"

My professor also taught me that cities also must adapt to survive. Inevitably, however, there are changes—perhaps trade patterns change, transportation routes alter, or laws are passed that can mark the end of prosperity for a region or town.

No mention was made in class, though, about the human issues. About the courageous people such as Liz Parenteau that stay and fight to prevent the decline and fall of their small towns. I thought of the story of the boy who stopped the leaky dike in Holland by jamming his finger in the hole. It seems that there aren't enough fingers to stop the economic leakage in many of these western outposts.

"We also struggle with the issue of Indian rights," she said. "We get along pretty well, but there are still resentments on both sides.

"It's too bad that we have these problems. I wish we all could cooperate as well as some of our ancestors. Did you fellows notice Lake Sakakawea today?" We nodded. It is a long lake—how could we miss the beauty of its shimmering blue color in the distance. But we didn't know the background of the name, so our friend told us about Sakakawea.

"Lewis and Clark's expedition headed to the Upper Missouri in the early 1800's. As you probably know, their expedition was the first effort by the United States to extend sovereignty over North Dakota. These explorers spent more time in North Dakota than any other area.

"While here, Lewis and Clark learned of Sakakawea, a young Shoshoni woman of seventeen. She had the misfortune of being captured by a war party of Hidatsas. A Frenchman living in the Knife River village had purchased her, and later married her. Lewis and Clark hired him as an interpreter to secure the services of his wife as a guide.

"Lewis and Clark were fortunate to have the services of Sakakawea. She was, according to Lewis, their only chance for a friendly negotiation with the Snake Indians. Clark, in particular, had a high regard for her, and later adopted her daughter after Sakakawea had died.

"For her part in the expedition, Sakakawea won undying fame with the American public. She has had more memorials dedicated to her than any other American woman."

Dave and I spent a few more minutes talking with our new friends, and then we headed towards town for dinner. We had a second chance to examine this small outpost.

Parshall appears to be breaking even in the struggle for survival. The civic leaders, for example, built the motel. Every successful town needs a nice motel, the thinking went. When we pedaled into town, we had seen a couple of museums that might attract a few tourists. The downtown shops looked relatively prosperous. Perhaps, with strong leadership, small towns can survive. We certainly feel better about Parshall's chances than we do about some of the other places we have passed.

Wanted: One Pharmacist

My employees and I have enjoyed the pleasure of your company in our little town and restaurant. We have enjoyed meeting, serving, and becoming friends with so many people from all over the country. We hope you enjoyed our hospitality and good food and hope to serve you and your friends again. Thank you.

—Menu from The Ranch House Restaurant, Towner, ND

U.S. Highway 2, called the "High Line," traverses the northern borders of Montana and North Dakota. The traffic is light, and the few drivers on the road are in a hurry to get to the larger cities such as Cut Bank, Williston, or Minot. The traffic is of little concern to us, however. In many places, it is a four lane highway with extra wide shoulders for additional security. It is almost as good as having a private bike path.

In many respects, U.S. 2 does seem indiscriminate. It allows motorists to bypass Harlem at 55 miles per hour, but leads right through the main streets of smaller towns like Chester. But mostly, the smaller towns and villages are bypassed, and in the minds of their citizens, the highway represents the sand–kicking beach bully. "If only the highway came through town," they say, "it would make all of the difference."

One such town is Towner, North Dakota. Like most of the communities on U.S. 2, Towner does offer a small eight room motel for the weary traveler. The manager smelled our desperation, and charged us thirty–five dollars for the room. The going rate in these small towns has been about thirty dollars. We didn't try to bargain.

"You had better hustle if you want something to eat," the manager said. Dave and I took his advice and made it to a pleasant family restaurant just before closing time.

We were the only diners in the Ranch House Restaurant. The owner's pride was evident in every corner. Country antiques and memorabilia added warmth to the spacious dining area. Blue gingham curtains framed each window, and handsome prints adorned the walls. The restaurant was clean, too, as if the governor was due in town.

As is our usual custom, Dave and I ordered half the items on the menu. Between courses, we talked to our waitress, a nice looking lady with a pleasant disposition.

"We lost our pharmacist two weeks ago," she said. "He moved away to a bigger city. Now we don't have a pharmacist."

A pharmacist in a drug store is something I have always taken for granted. You show up, turn in a prescription, and thirty minutes later, you get your medicine. I have never considered other possibilities.

"I don't know what we are going to do," she continued. "We've been advertising for a replacement, but so far we've had no luck. It's tough getting someone to move here. Towner is a small town, and we don't have big city attractions. The highway certainly didn't help.

"I worry about Towner," she said. "You lose your pharmacist, and people start driving to the next town to get prescriptions. Next thing you know, they wonder why they are driving somewhere for something as simple as a prescription. You can't really blame them for moving."

I sympathized with the plight of this small town. Who would move here? I can't imagine a young college graduate living and working in Towner. For that matter, I can't imagine anyone really moving here.

It is an accepted fact that there is a migration of the young from the Towners and Harlems to the larger metropolitan areas. Perhaps the constant bombardment of television has convinced the younger generation that big city life is the preferred life-style.

In the morning, we went back to the Ranch House for breakfast. Again, we were the only diners, even the usual coffee drinkers were absent. This is a first for our trip. We have grown accustomed to the restaurants and cafes being the social center of the small towns. I wonder how the restaurant will survive.

After a delicious breakfast of french toast, crisp bacon, and fried eggs, Dave and I wandered back to the kitchen area to meet the owner, Judy Schell, and express our thanks for the excellent food. She is, as we expected, a warm, outgoing person, with a pleasant smile on her face. We have the feeling that she is happy to be running her restaurant.

*   *   *

"These small towns remind me of my own home town," Dave said. "I grew up in McCormick, South Carolina, during a period when most of my friends graduated from high school and moved away. When I went away to college, I didn't have much hope for my hometown. People were leaving, businesses were closing, and the town was dying. My dad, though, was committed to the community, and never thought of leaving. He did his best to improve things, and motivated others to do the same. In fact, when he retired from his business, the town elected him mayor. During that time, things turned around. New businesses moved in, a lake front community was formed, and young people became more involved in politics and community service. Perhaps they saw there was hope. During the 1980's, McCormick thrived. I think Liz is right. A single individual can make a tremendous difference. It sure did for McCormick, and maybe it will for Harlem."

I met Dave's dad a few years ago, and, although I was impressed with his friendliness, I felt that there was even more to the man. There was a sense of purpose and a desire to make a difference.

"I think my dad would like Liz Parenteau." Dave said. "She, too, has a strong commitment to the community. They would have a great time comparing notes. You see, twenty years ago, Interstate 20 had just been finished and diverted the truckers around McCormick. Sounds a lot like the U.S. 2 argument we've heard in these parts."

How badly my college professor erred in not accounting for the strength and impact of the determined individual. The difference these people make cannot be factored into any statistical equation. I doubt that any professor, safely snug in a tenured office in a remote university, can possibly understand the impact made possible by one person with a deeply held conviction.

Dave and Ricky reach the summit at Washingon Pass

Dave, near Ione, Washington, with his seriously loaded bike

Bill, ready to depart Bull Lake Guest Ranch, Bull Lake, Montana

Ricky returns! Glacier National Park, Montana

Bill and Liz Parenteau,
Harlem Montana

The Geographical Center of North America,
Rugby, North Dakota

Big Sky Country, near New Town, North Dakota

Bill, Paul, and Babe, Bemidji, Minnesota

The narrator, crossing the Mississippi River, near its headwaters in Itasco State Park, Minnesota

Dave Fooshe and Dave Lorenz, Sterling Illinois

Dave, deep in Illinois corn country

The Popsicle Gang strikes again, near Pontiac, Illinois

The Valley of the Shadow, Backroads, Indiana

The Ohio River, near Veevay, Indiana

Farmer Dave in Kentucky

Dave, The Breaks Interstate Park, Virginia

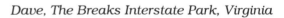

Father Ralph, The Breaks Interstate Park, Virginia

Dave celebrates the final state crossing, near Oxford, North Carolina

New Bern, North Carolina

Part Four

The River Run

Ya, I think I kin halp

Failed Dreams

Wisconsin

Minnesota

Who-dood in
Harper's Ferry

West of the diagonal line marks the
flat part of Iowa. Long-ago, glaciers
smoothed the land in this part of the
state. Of course, Dave & I didn't cycle there.

Dave has a
great idea

Iowa

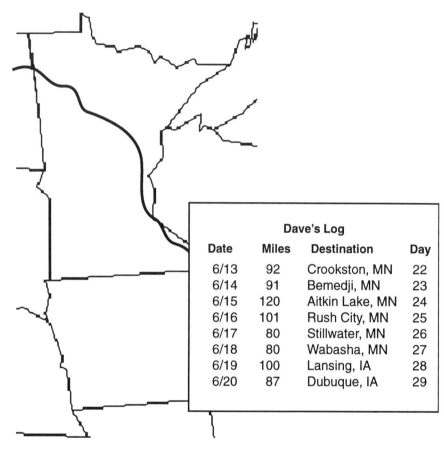

Dave's Log			
Date	**Miles**	**Destination**	**Day**
6/13	92	Crookston, MN	22
6/14	91	Bemedji, MN	23
6/15	120	Aitkin Lake, MN	24
6/16	101	Rush City, MN	25
6/17	80	Stillwater, MN	26
6/18	80	Wabasha, MN	27
6/19	100	Lansing, IA	28
6/20	87	Dubuque, IA	29

Scenery: ★★★★★
The scenic St. Croix and Mississippi Rivers were constant companions.

Roads: ★★
Downright painful. Sometimes the roads were so rough, it took an hour after cycling for my bottom to stop shaking like half–frozen Jello.

People: ★★★★
Only our encounters with the larger, more indifferent cities kept this region from obtaining the coveted, and much talked about, Fitzpatrick and Fooshe Five Star rating.

Weather: ★★
It was so hot, all we had to do was pour some Taster's Choice in our water bottles to make piping hot coffee.

Winds of Change

Old longings nomadic leap,
Chafing at custom's chain;
Again from its brumal sleep
Wakens the ferine strain.

—Jack London,
The Call of the Wild

I'll never forget Professor Bob. He had a most annoying habit. After watching a movie, or reading a book, he would insist on describing the event using some ridiculous, obscure symbolism. He cornered me one afternoon in class and asked me what I thought of *Moby Dick*.

"Not a bad story," I responded, "although, it was obvious from the start that the fish was going to get Ahab. Melville should have taken a page from Poe and put in more suspense. It was pretty good for a fish story though."

My last comment generated a large amount of laughter from the class. They too, were laughing at the absurdity. English professors often take things to extremes.

I wonder what symbolism Professor Bob might have used to describe the violent storms that met us at the border of Minnesota and North Dakota.

*   *   *

"Stop, stop!" Dave screamed at me. A bolt of lightning struck near the highway, no more than a mile in the distance. Despite near tornadic winds that whipped us along at speeds close to forty miles per hour, we had lost our desperate race to the town of Crookston, Minnesota. We dropped our bikes and raced on foot towards a distant barn, hoping that it was open.

The barn doors were locked.

The only low–lying area was a four foot ditch that followed the main highway. We eyed this "safe" spot suspiciously—low hanging power lines directly above it would make short work of a skinny redhead and an analytical engineer. With no place else to go, we hit the ditch, and watched in awe the Battle of Crookston.

It was a hellish storm that would make even Dante blush. Dark clouds swirled and twisted in random patterns. Sheets of rain pelted indiscriminately. While Dave and I stayed relatively dry, we could see that the town of Crookston, a scant mile or two down the road, was getting pulverized. In a little over thirty minutes, Dave and I fished our bikes out of the ditch, and pedaled into town. It was not until the morning paper that we learned the full extent of the storm's wrath.

Wall of hail shreds beautiful corn crop
4" of rain fell like a blanket
Lightning strike kills 1, hurts 5 at U.S. Open
Grand Forks Herald,
(Grand Forks, Minnesota)

The day was memorable, however, in more ways than the storm. We had finally exited the plains. To Dave, this was a defining moment, every bit as important as the election of Ronald Reagan as president. Dave told me how he felt about it.

"The lack of scenery really wore on my nerves. I like to look at different pictures now and then. I felt like I was looking at the same photo album day after day."

I reminded Dave of the subtle beauty of the land—the Bears Paw Mountains, Lake Sakakawea, and the sometimes inspiring emerald green hills. The people were unique, far different than any group I have ever met. The solemn lonely battlers we encountered all had a haunting, inescapable love of the land. Does this barren, often foreboding region attract this personality, or does the land somehow impose its will, dictating even moods and emotions?

"Chester, Montana," said Dave, "summed up the whole experience for me. Remember we got up early, and walked down to the town cafe? The ranchers and farmers were already there drinking coffee and talking about the night's rain. A man in his fifties from a nearby table got up and served us coffee. After he filled our cups, he explained that they all pitched in to help Jim, the owner, who would be with us in a minute. In five minutes Jim did indeed appear to take our order. He stopped on the way into the kitchen, put on his cook's hat, and reappeared shortly with our breakfast. His cashier's hat was on when we paid for our meals. I bet his owner's hat was on when he mopped up at night."

I gave Dave a perfunctory nod. I was brooding about the storm, the plains, and for some inextricable reason, Professor Bob. The old sonofabitch was at it again.

"Bill, you stupid amoeba, it was not just a storm, it was an epic transitional event. Happening as it did, right on the border of North Dakota and Minnesota was more than mere coincidence.

"Obviously, the plains are symbolic of the dark, brooding side of your conscience—that part of all of us that wants to be, in your crude words, 'left the hell alone.'"

I nodded. That part sounded like me.

The English professor continued. "The winds at the border can also be interpreted as symbolic of the dichotomy of your personality—your simultaneous resistance and attraction to this part of yourself. You do indeed want to be blown back into the part of the country where you perceive life to be simpler. But not at the expense of the finer things in life.

"The tornadic winds are also symbolic of the spiritual turmoil that your soul has experienced. The immense physical struggle of the air masses as you entered Minnesota and left North Dakota and Montana, can be seen, in proper context, as being representative of the dramatic cleansing of your soul. The harsh stark, brooding reality of the plains has cleansed your old soul, leaving you free to find your new soul in the coming days."

I couldn't help myself. "Then again, Bob, maybe it was just a big old storm."

Arly

Under a spreading chestnut–tree
The village smithy stands;
The smith, a mighty man is he
With large and sinewy hands;
And the muscles of his brawny arms
Are strong as iron bands.

—Henry Wadsworth Longfellow,
The Village Blacksmith,

"I'll be glad to give you a ride to Steinberg's Welding & Fabrication. It shouldn't take long, Fosston is just a few miles down the road. Of course, they only do heavy welding there, and might not be able to fix your bike. What did you say the problem was again?"

"The frame is cracked," Dave responded, "and unless I can get it fixed, it's going to end our trip. Would you mind giving me a ride?"

"Not at all, glad to help out," Jim said. "It's not like I have anything else to do today, and besides, I need to go there anyway to pick up my last paycheck. I got laid off two weeks ago from the local dairy. I don't know what I'm going to do to support my wife and two kids."

"Oh," said Dave, "I'm sorry."

We carefully placed Dave's bike and gear into the back of the pickup and Dave and Jim drove east on U.S. 2. Not wanting to miss any miles, I decided to pedal the eight miles to Fosston.

Barely an hour from Crookston we had crossed some railroad tracks. Shortly after, Dave asked me to drop back and look at his rear wheel. He thought he had broken another spoke.

This was no broken spoke. His bike was wobbling like a dying top. It appeared to be made of two pieces with a single loose screw holding the halves together. It didn't take Dave long to locate the problem. The frame had cracked near the rear axle bracket.

I looked at Dave, "Since the start of the trip, you've been flying like a bat out of hell over every single railroad track. It might not have been so bad if you hadn't overpacked by fifty pounds. I don't know why you look so surprised."

I looked at Dave's expression again and decided not to say that.

Instead, I said, "What bad luck. It's only a matter of time before it happens to me. I should probably get my frame checked."

Finding a bike shop in the back roads of Minnesota was out of the question. Our only chance was to get the frame welded back together.

But where?

Our first stop had been a small town with a single service station. It was a busy shop, but despite the activity, the owner and another employee came over and examined the bike.

"Well, we can't do anything with your bike," the owner had said. "We only do rough welding work here, so we'd be afraid to touch it. But Jim here will give you a lift to Fosston, and there's a commercial welding shop up there. They might be able to help. Good luck."

*   *   *

It took me about thirty minutes to reach Fosston. I stopped at a small convenience store, picked up some lunch items, and caught up with Dave in front of the welding shop.

"Hi, are you Arly?" Dave questioned the large Swede who had just roared up on, well, a Harley. He had been waiting for almost an hour outside of Steinberg's.

"Sure ahm, how can ay hilp ya?"

"My frame is cracked and we're bicycling across the country. Think you can weld it back?" Dave pleaded, his voice showing a trace of desperation.

"Let's have a look, I've ne'er done anything like this before." Arly responded in his soft Scandinavian accent—the kind you would expect from an Arly.

Arly had plenty of help, too. At least seven of the dozen or so welders at Steinberg's were staring at Dave's puny touring bike. Large commercial welding projects were left unattended for at least fifteen minutes as each welder gave his opinion of what needed to be done. Make no mistake, though, this was Arly's project. The manager had told us he was the best man for the job.

"Yir bike is surely made of'n alloy, I don't know what'll happen if I weld it," said Arly. We had no choice. Dave told him to take his best shot, and spare no expense.

Torches were lit, the mask was donned, and Arly began to expertly paint a fine bond of steel across the fractured joint. Other welders came by to check on the progress. I noticed Dave was sweating—I wasn't sure if he was nervous about the welding or the size of the repair bill. After about an hour of work, the job was finished.

"It should work," Arly said, "take 'er for a ride."

Arly and I watched Dave nervously pedal away. I wanted to say, "Dave watch out for the tracks," but decided not to. Instead, I said, "Let 'er rip, buddy!"

In five minutes, Dave returned with a broad grin. The only remaining issue was the charge for Arly's time, material, expertise, seven commercial welders' advice, and the time taken away from the other projects. I slowly walked away from Dave because the potential size of the bill had me concerned. He had that "I might need a loan" look on his face.

Arly looked carefully at the clock, scribbled a few numbers on a pad of paper, banged for long time on his calculator and said, "Six dollars."

Dave and I went numb—we hadn't been this stunned since we encountered the leggy blonde back in Nowhere, Montana. Not that she made a lasting impression or anything. We both guessed the bill would be at least $200.

Dave quickly ripped out a twenty dollar bill and Arly began to make change.

"Not necessary! Not necessary!" Dave screamed.

"Well, lit me getya a receipt thin?" Arly said.

"Not necessary," Dave said. "No reason at all for a receipt."

We thanked Arly many times, and waved good–bye to the welders that had come by to help. Perhaps we had provided them with a story or two for their dinner table.

With a major crisis behind us, we continued our journey east on Highway 2.

The Fishing Village Blues

I have learned this, at least, by my experiment; that if one advances confidently in the direction of his dreams, and endeavors to live the life which he has imagined, he will meet with a success unexpected in common hours.

—Henry David Thoreau

Dave and I wearily pedaled the last mile into Sandy Lake Lodge. We had left the resort town of Bemidji in the morning, and pedaled through the small fishing villages of the Chippewa National Forest. Cass Lake, Bena and Ball Club all cling to Lake Winnibigoshish and Leech Lake for their economic survival. It looked to me like they might be losing their grip.

The highlight of the afternoon was when Dave and I crossed the Mississippi River near its headwaters in Itasca State Park. We are yet another landmark closer to the North Carolina coast. This is not the last time we will cross the river—it will be our constant companion for the next week or so.

Dave opened the door to the lodge and spoke to the owner.

"Any cabins left?" he asked Tom, the proprietor.

"No, it's Saturday night and they're all rented," he replied.

"What about campsites?" I asked, eyeing the large grassy area out near the playground.

"No, the campsites are full, too," he replied.

"Would you mind if we pitched our tent out by the playground?" I asked, desperately.

"Let me check with my wife, Mary." he replied.

"Bicycling across the country? Of course they can camp near the playground." Mary was just entering the office and had overheard part of our conversation.

"Of course you can," said Tom.

Now there's a real boss.

*　　　*　　　*

Tom and Mary were congenial hosts and offered to bake the frozen pizzas we selected from the freezer. Having pedaled a hundred and twenty miles—a record for us—we inquired about a six pack of beer. Unfortunately, they did not sell this vital necessity. Sensing our disappointment, Tom went back to his refrigerator, and whipped out a couple of cold Budweisers. He freshened his own drink and joined us at the table to tell us about his lodge.

"This property is my true love. I bought it twenty years ago while employed with the Great Northern Railroad, and developed it as a hobby until I retired a few years ago. I had hoped that this would provide a full time income. Unfortunately, we're really too far from the Twin Cities for day travellers, so we depend mostly on the weekend trade. Plus, the season is short. We're lucky if we get four full months.

"All my life, I have dreamed of owning my own place on the lake. And now that I have it, I wonder if it's really worth it. It's a lot of hard work for very few dollars."

I came to the lightning conclusion that this was not the guy to help me find my lost soul. How depressing. You work all your life for what you want, and then once you get it, you decide it wasn't worth the fight?

We were briefly interrupted by the arrival of several guests. A grandfather and his two young grandsons came in to show Tom their catch. The smaller boy, no more than eight years old, proudly held up a large walleye. The other boy had also met with success, and held up a string of smaller fish. The grandfather didn't have any fish, but that didn't seem to be important. After they left, Tom continued his thoughts.

"You guys are really lucky to be able to take such a trip. I would love to be able to do something like that. Not on a bike, of course, but maybe a motorhome."

We have heard this refrain from many people during our trip, but this was different. Tom's comments were heartfelt—we sensed a longing on his part to live our dream, to forget, ever so briefly, that his dream had not turned out as he had hoped. He disappeared for a minute, and came back with a couple more beers for us. He freshened his scotch and sat back down. There was no charge for the drinks.

"Lots of people have told us how lucky we are," Dave said. "Bill and I know how lucky we are to realize our dreams. It doesn't always turn out that way."

Tom nodded his head.

Dave continued. "Just this morning, for example, we were forced to pull off the road—I had broken a spoke that needed attention. We pulled into an abandoned motel along the shore of Winnibigoshish Lake and were confronted by a rough–looking drunk asking for a three dollar handout. I'm sure he once had his dreams.

"The abandoned motel consisted of a dozen separate cottages, each of which were rotting from neglect. The windows were shattered—fragments of glass were still scattered in the overgrown yard. A few of the doors remained on their hinges, though, most had rotted away. The faded white and green colors left the impression of better days past. Only the gas pumps looked indifferent to the passing years. The broken sign out front said 'The Fishing Village.'

"It too, was once somebody's dream."

Tom was quiet for a minute after listening to Dave's story. Perhaps he was wondering if his lodge might suffer a similar fate.

We spent a while longer talking with Tom about the many people and places we have seen along the way. Several times he inquired about the cost of the trip. For those who ask, we give the standard reply, "This is a once in a lifetime trip and we aren't going to worry about the cost."

Tom shook his head, took a last sip, and said good night.

*   *   *

We returned to our tent on the playground. Dave and I wrote a few lines in our diaries, and turned in for the night.

For the first time since the beginning of the trip, I was able to relax inside a tent. A warm breeze rustled the leaves of the hardwoods that were down by the lake. The buzz of the mosquitoes added a certain ethereal quality to the night. Then the evocative cry of the loons joined the symphony. I was about to drift off to a pleasant sleep when...

An unscrupulous New Yorker—don't ask me how, I just know—turned on a blaring rock and roll station.

One man's heaven is another man's hell.

I didn't get any sleep and was quite crabby in the morning.

American Pie

"For the truckers cruise over the surface of the nation without being a part of it. Quite often I sat with these men and listened to their talk and then asked questions. I soon learned not to expect knowledge of the country they passed through. Except for the truck stops, they had no contact with it. It was driven home to me how like sailors they were. I remember when I first went to sea being astonished that the men who sailed over the world and touched the ports to the strange and exotic had little contact with that world."

—John Steinbeck,
Travels with Charley, In Search of America

Forty miles east of Minneapolis is as close to a major city as Dave and I plan to pedal. We took a southern route from Aitkin Lake this morning, and were forced to cycle over twenty–five miles on a narrow two lane road. The highway was busy carrying the weekend traffic to and from the nearby recreational lakes. In a hurry to reach their destinations, the cars, many hauling speed boats, raced by at speeds well over sixty m.p.h.

As if this wasn't enough, we also had to contend with narrow shoulders, and a hot southeasterly wind. Our tempers got the better of us, and after screaming invectives at a couple of cars, we exited onto some unmarked county roads. Surprisingly, we didn't get lost.

It was a brief respite from urban America, though. Late in the afternoon, we ended our day at a small crossroads town that has no name. It is one of those places that exists only to service traffic from a nearby interstate, and is probably known by a number as in "Officer O'Reilly, please respond to a code 35 at exit 33."

There were two greasy spoons, one bar, one large service station, and one motel.

Despite the "No Vacancy" sign, Dave and I walked into the office. Even though it was almost 7:00 p.m., there were no cars in the newly paved parking lot. Dave did the talking.

"Got a room for the night?" he asked.

"Plenty of room," the owner said. "Absolutely slowest day of the year. Can't understand it—yesterday was like this, too."

"Uhh, your No Vacancy sign is on," Dave said.

"Damn! Not again!" the owner said, "Damn! Damn! Damn!"

After taking showers, we headed out for dinner. For the first time, I was about to experience America through the eyes of a truck driver.

*   *   *

"Whatcha want?"

Our waitress was a lady in her sixties, an earthy kind of woman. Despite the crowd in the restaurant, she was the only waitress. I was about to order when...

Swat! She took a wild swing at a nearby fly. Blap! She got the next one. "Damn flies really irritate me," she said, more annoyed than pleased at her success.

"Oh yes," I said.

Cigarette smoke hung in the air. The smell of burnt oil mixed with the smoke to create a green haze of acid clouds. Most of the menu items were fried dishes with little nutritional value.

"I'll have a bowl of soup, the meat loaf, a baked potato, green beans, and a tossed salad," I said, thinking this would be somewhat better than the fried dinners.

"Baked potato?" she said. "You mean mashed potatoes!"

"No ma'am, I want a baked potato," I repeated.

"Baked potato? Are you sure you want a baked potato? Everybody orders mashed potatoes with meat loaf. I'll go ahead and order you mashed potatoes." She jotted in her pad and took another swipe at a fly.

I have always been skeptical of mashed potatoes in cheap restaurants. I know they don't use real potatoes. Instead of serving healthy, hearty, potassium filled potatoes from Idaho, they serve "potatoes" made from plastic bags of chemical flakes. These flakes have no relation to real potatoes, and are probably manufactured in Newark, New Jersey.

"I want a baked potato, and that's all there is to it." I fairly screamed this order at the waitress. Several nearby diners stared at me. The waitress slunk off with the order.

Dave and I had a few minutes to absorb the surroundings. It was evident that the restaurant got a good deal on dull green items. Furnishings, plates, cooking machines, and curtains. All dull green. Even the haze above our heads was a dull green. The haze was perpetuated by the presence of a large number of smokers, all of whom looked like truck drivers.

This was our first encounter with a truck stop diner. Until now, we have successfully avoided these types of establishments. Our route has taken us through small towns populated with friendly people who have been willing to spend a few moments with us and offer a glimpse of their community. This diner is only in business for the interstate trade. "Get 'em in and get 'em out" is clearly their purpose. No one lingers over coffee, pie and conversation.

Our waitress served our meal. It looked green. Perhaps I look green, too. Is it Venus where light gets trapped and reflected, and everything looks to be the same color? I glanced again at the smoke above us.

We gulped our dinner. To prove her point, our waitress served me a tiny, overcooked, shriveled baked potato. The gravy on the meatloaf was a dull gray, actually blending in nicely with the green hues. The limp green beans looked as tired and worn as the furniture.

The waitress brought the check. "Excuse me ma'am, we would like to order dessert," I said. I startled her. Perhaps she thought the baked potato scared me off.

"You want dessert, too?" she replied, somewhat annoyed.

I stood up. This was the last straw.

"Let's be honest for just a minute, lady. Are you here to make money? If you are, let me explain a few things to you. The bigger the bill, the higher the tip. Write that down. This is Economics 101. And what this means to you, (and here I pointed at her) is that you will make more money by selling me dessert."

I continued, "And another thing. Why were we served oleo and non–dairy creamer? This is the land of the dairy farm." I pointed to some cows out the window. "I have yet to see a cow that gives oleo. How do you expect the farmers in Minnesota to survive when you people serve chemically produced, artificially enhanced, superficially preserved "food" from places like Bayonne, New Jersey."

She repeated her question, "Do you want dessert?"

"Yes ma'am. We'd like some of your fine apple pie and a scoop of your delicious vanilla ice cream."

She brought us apple pie from a cardboard box with Cool Whip on top. Dave and I finished our dessert, paid our bill, and headed back to the motel. Neither of us spoke for a few minutes—we were trying to comprehend what we had just been through.

Dave finally broke the silence, "There's only one good thing about bad service, Bill."

"Please tell me," I said.

"It doesn't bother me as much when I don't leave a tip."

*   *   *

To make up for the Bad Diner disaster, Dave and I pedaled ten miles the next morning and enjoyed breakfast at the Grant Inn.

The Grant Inn is an historic building dating back to the 1800's. Drummers—another word for salesmen—stayed here during their trips down the St. Croix River, and met in the bar to talk about their accounts. Back then, the rooms only had only a chair, a bed, and a Gideon's Bible.

Our breakfast at the Grant Inn was first rate. My pancakes were stuffed with plump blueberries and topped with whipped butter and warm maple syrup. Dave's eggs were superb, and he claimed his pecan waffle was the best he'd ever had. We stuffed our panniers with several homemade raspberry pastries, left the Grant Inn, and continued our southeastern path through Minnesota.

Comfort Zones

When Thales was asked...
"What was difficult?" he said,
"To know one's self."
And What was easy?
"To advise another."

—Diogenes Laertius

While leaning on the steel rail of the bridge that would lead us from Minnesota into Prescott, Wisconsin, we enjoyed the natural beauty of the St. Croix and Mississippi Rivers. These two historic rivers intersect at this point, with the latter now responsible for the solo journey down to the Gulf of Mexico.

It had been a beautiful ride in the morning. On both sides of the river, dark red barns, and white clapboard homes speak of rich land and hard working people. It was tough biking though—a stiff breeze, challenging hills, and a scorching day gradually wore us down. We were delayed twice in the morning—once by an intense thunderstorm, and then we got lost by following bad directions. Dave was now getting it out of his system.

"ZOI, Bill," he said. "Zone of Indifference."

I nodded like I understood. If someone wants to pull their shirttail out, you let them.

"I have been amazed on this trip at the number of people that don't know the directions, landmarks, or highways to the next town. That guy outside of Stillwater couldn't give us directions to the main highway, and he had lived there all his life. His lousy directions took us at least an hour out of our way.

"Or, how about that thirty–year–old lady back in Surrey, North Dakota? We thought the highway fifty yards away was U.S. 2, but when we asked for her confirmation, she shook her head and said 'I don't know, I really don't travel much.'"

I remembered her. When I asked her where she was from, she said, "Surrey."

"Oh yes" I had said, "oh yes."

128

Dave wasn't through pulling out his shirttail. He was fully committed to this line of thought, and stopping him now would do no good.

"There are other ways that people limit themselves. Remember that lady that let us stay in her garage this morning?"

"Yes," I said. A brief, intense thunderstorm had caused us to seek shelter, and with a wave of her hand, the woman had given us permission to go into her large, three car garage. It was littered with the toys of the well–to–do, including golf clubs, snow skis, and tennis rackets. Also in the garage was a brand new white Cadillac.

After the storm abated, the woman came out to her car. She had an appointment in town.

"Where are you guys headed?" she asked.

"Cross country ma'am," I responded. "We're riding our bikes across the country."

"I'm so embarrassed," she said. "If I had known that, I would have invited you in."

I realized this lady couldn't help me with my lost soul. There is something in the Bible about helping people in need. It doesn't go into a lot of detail about what constitutes "in need," however. Maybe it's time these loopholes are tidied up. For example, are ragged cyclists dodging hellish storms to be considered "in need?" I think so. The "help" part of it should be spelled out, too. Is providing a garage enough, or should we have expected milk and cookies, too?

"That lady," Dave said, "was obviously well educated and articulate. I am sure she could have given us directions to the next town. But she was not willing to stretch as a person and expose herself to a different experience, such as venturing to say hello to two cyclists. That's not much better than living your entire life within a two block area of your home. What's happened to the spirit of adventure in America! We must break out of our comfort zones."

I didn't respond to Dave's ramblings. I had other problems.

Back in Stillwater, they had laughed at my underwear. We always hang our laundry on the back of our bikes to dry. For some reason, a crowd of yuppies, all dressed in striped shirts, khaki pants, and Dockers, found my luggage amusing.

Of course, I may have been overly sensitive. The ten mile stretch leading into Stillwater had been a tough one for me, and I was in no mood to be ridiculed. Struggling with steep hills and a merciless headwind, I had been further tortured by two flat tires and empty water bottles.

The town didn't help. Stillwater is the consummate tourist trap with fancy restaurants and exclusive hotels. Expensive automobiles jammed the narrow streets and made safe cycling nearly impossible. After almost four weeks of small towns and lonesome highways, we were not prepared for this onslaught of civilization.

I felt like screaming, "Die, yuppie scum" to the underwear baiters, but I didn't. I could only hope they would choke on their chicken breast primavera or a potted fern would fall on their pointed heads.

The Anderson House

The Historic Anderson House welcomes you to gracious dining in the tradition of Pennsylvania Dutch Congeniality, Generous Country Cooking and the charm of an 18th Century Inn. Step back into yesterday. when chivalry was legend, guests were pampered, and hospitality an art.

—Brochure from the Anderson House, Wabasha, MN

For the first time during the trip, Dave and I were conscious of our appearance as we entered the lobby of the Anderson House. We usually pull into small, sometimes rundown motels, and never give a thought to our appearance. We suspect we smell bad, but never know for sure. Kind of like working in a chemistry lab. After a while, you tend to forget you smell like sulfur dioxide. But this was no rundown motel.

There was nothing to suggest that such a beautiful old establishment might be located in this small town. From all outward appearances, Wabasha, Minnesota is like many of the other small, nondescript places we have visited. There are a couple of gas stations, several shops, and a few slow moving pedestrians. From our initial review, the only selling point to this small town is its location on the banks of the Mississippi River.

It had been a dazzling afternoon of cycling, many times we rode directly along the Mississippi. It is no longer the puny, wandering, adolescent of previous days. Instead, it has matured into a rippling young adult. Towering limestone bluffs on both the Minnesota and Wisconsin sides gave the river the proper framing. The blue sky, with just the right amount of soft white clouds, added the proper texture.

*   *   *

"Welcome to the Anderson House," Jeanne Hall greeted us as if we were executives in three piece suits. Encouraged, Dave and I signed in.

The Anderson House is Minnesota's oldest operating hotel, and is included in the National Registry of Historic Places. All of the rooms have antiques that date back to the 1850's. The present innkeepers, John, Gayla, and Jeanne Hall are the fourth generation to own and operate the Anderson House.

It was as if the Anderson House received cross country cyclists every day. Jeanne led us around the side of the building and held the doors while we secured our bikes inside the sun room. The tables in the room had already been set with fine linen and glistening crystal. Our dirty bikes looked out of place—not unlike their owners.

"You boys would probably like a good dinner," Jeanne said; "our dining room stays open 'til 9:00 p.m. You have time for a bath (a not so subtle hint!) and a change of clothes, so why don't you plan on joining us?"

She got no argument. On the way to our rooms, we noted the many fine antiques that lined the hallways. Our European style rooms also have period antiques, adding a Victorian charm to our surroundings.

Dinner was memorable. Ice cold beer, shrimp appetizers, five different kinds of homemade breads, crispy onion rings, and fresh green salads whetted our appetites for the thick slabs of steak and man–sized baked potatoes. We had huge portions of homemade strawberry ice cream and rhubarb pie for dessert. The riverboat barons never had it so good. Even the music was appropriate; "Old Man River" was playing in the background.

We got up from the table, and with wobbly legs and glazed eyes, we headed up to our rooms. I picked up a leaflet on the Anderson House. It told of other interesting services.

As in Grandma Anderson's day, shoes left outside the door are meticulously shined. If you complain about cold feet, then they will quickly be warmed by a hot brick for your bed, carefully presented in a quilted envelope. If you're ailing? A mustard plaster will be delivered for your cold with instructions for use. If you are here during Christmas, you'll find Christmas trees all over the house. New Year's will find champagne delivered to your room, and if you wander in on April 30th, you'll find a May Basket on your door. The ever-filled cookie jar is still present at the front desk.

But that isn't the best part.

If you make the proper arrangements when booking your room, you can get custody of one of the hotel's fifteen cats during your stay, for no extra charge. Many of the guests use the felines for bed warmers!

"We give them the cat and the litter box and some food," said Jeanne. "They might be anyone from a family with a child to a young woman traveling alone. "Also honeymoon couples: That just slays us—I'd think they would have other interests."

That slayed me too. A honeymoon couple sharing their room with a cat. I turned out the light and drowsily considered the possibilities. Maybe it was an older couple. Or maybe the couple wasn't getting along, and they talked to each other through the cat. No telling for sure.

The Intrepid Reporters

*Nature has given women so much power
that the law has wisely given them little.*

—Samuel Johnson
(1709 – 1784)

"Reporters, eh? I thought you ladies looked a little different."

The four ladies, all in their sixties and seventies, greeted my comment with polite laughter. They had been staring at Dave and me for at least thirty minutes—from time to time they whispered to each other and then turned to look at us some more. Finally, the oldest one tested the water.

"You boys aren't from around here, are you?"

Reporters can be so insightful and intuitive. I wonder what gave us away? Was it the maps that were spread across the table? Was it the triple cholesterol, double–decker breakfast we each consumed? Or maybe it is the worn haggard look that Dave and I have had on our faces since crossing the Minnesota–Iowa border. Every day has been at least ninety degrees with a consistent pattern of hot and humid head-winds.

"No ma'am, we're not from here. My friend is from Los Angeles and I'm from South Carolina. We are cycling across the country and stopped here for breakfast."

It wasn't as if we had any place else to stop. According to our maps, Harpers Ferry, Iowa was the only town within twenty miles that offered any chance for breakfast. We had already climbed two of the toughest grades of the trip and were long past being ready to eat.

My comments generated great interest among the reporters. The enthusiasm was contagious—yes, a write–up in the local newspaper would be nice. Who knows, maybe we'll make the front page. Pictures, yes! AP! UPI! Yes! Yes! We decided to linger and answer their questions.

"Why do it?" they asked me.

"My first objective is to find my soul. Oh, sure, I want to see the country, and indeed that is part of my motive, but mostly I want to get away from it all, and discover the 'real me'."

I launched into a few of my favorite stories. Being the salesman, I enjoy telling stories and am naturally inclined to minor embellishment. And like any good salesman, the more stories I tell, the more stories I want to tell. In short, I gave these ladies a lengthy description of our entire journey.

Dave chimed in with his thoughts, "To see the country is one thing, but this is an opportunity of a lifetime. So many people we encounter respond by saying that this is something they always wanted to do. How often do you get to do something you always wanted to do? The opportunity presented itself, and, so, here we are in Harper's Ferry, Iowa, having breakfast and talking to you all."

Dave elaborated on a few of his favorite stories.

Close to an hour later, I noticed something disturbing. Nobody was taking notes. There were no tape recorders present, either. On closer examination, these ladies didn't really fit the image of intrepid newspaper reporters. How will they get our story straight?

"Excuse me, ladies. None of you are taking notes. How in the world will you remember all of our experiences?"

I said this with a bright smile on my face because I didn't want to appear offensive.

"We're agricultural reporters."

I went berserk. "I want each of you to know that we are way behind schedule because of this. You should have told us you were agricultural reporters. We wouldn't have wasted so much time."

I really didn't say that. I really said, "How wonderful. I bet you do a great job. We would love to have our names in your excellent publication. Let me help you with the spelling of Fitzpatrick and Fooshe."

An hour behind schedule, and grumpy after being taken in by the blue–haired grannies, we paid our bill and left Harper's Ferry.

A Friendly Bar

The world is so full of a number of things
I'm sure we should all be as happy as kings.

—Robert Louis Stevenson,
Happy Thought

Before going into the bar and restaurant to refill our water bottles, Dave and I stared at yet another spectacular end–of–the–day scene. We gazed at the hazy green farmland in the distant valleys, the Mississippi snaking its way through the rolling hills, and the Wisconsin dairy farms sitting proudly above the eastern shore of the lazy river. While relaxing, we remembered the descent into the Okanogan Valley, the sudden, startling view of the Canadian Rockies on the way into Eureka, and the special memory of our late afternoon entrance into Apgar, and Lake McDonald.

After a long, hot, torturous day, we deserved a reward. The climb up to Ball Town was the eighth major climb of the day in this supposedly flat farming state.

What are these hills doing in Iowa? Glaciers descending from the north had smoothed the land we have been riding through. In northeastern Iowa, however, the glaciers left the land untouched. It was up to the Mississippi to cut gorges in the mountainous terrain—also known as bluffs. Occasionally, a city or town was found nestled between the bluffs and the historic river, towns such as Lansing, Harper's Ferry, Millville, and Buena Vista. The highway follows the river for a few miles, and then heads abruptly into the hills. One memorable grade was eight percent—the sharpest incline of the trip. With the ninety–five degree temperature and ninety percent humidity, Dave and I were drained at the end of the day.

*   *   *

An older crowd was sitting at the bar, enjoying a drink or two before dinner. Genuine, hearty laughter filled the room—it was contagious. Dave and I seated ourselves at the bar, and for the first time, we ordered a cold beer before the end of the day.

"I can tell you boys have been traveling a few miles. Well, tell us, doesn't Iowa have the friendliest people?"

The speaker was a well–dressed gentleman, about fifty years old. He asked the question with a big smile and laughter in his eyes. A number of people turned and looked at us, eagerly awaiting our response. I took his question seriously.

"Iowa has great people," I answered, "but the people we have met in other states have been friendly, too. It has reaffirmed our faith in the whole country."

It's the simple courtesies that make all the difference. Only an hour earlier, Dave and I stopped at a small auto repair shop for water. It was a nondescript shop located at the intersection of two county roads. You needn't bother looking for the attached gift shop. And no, it was not the type of place that keeps hot coffee and a color television available for waiting customers.

Dave and I walked into the small office. A middle–aged man was there, hunched over some paperwork. It was an office that only a mechanic could appreciate. Papers everywhere, a few styrofoam coffee cups, an ashtray with plenty of butts, and last year's Midas muffler calendar. The occupant looked like his office.

We asked if we could fill our water bottles with his water. It was the middle of the day, we knew he was busy, could he point us to the men's room?

"You fellas need colder water than that, follow me," he said. He dropped his work, stepped outside, and led us to a well with a hand pump, located not far from the neat, white house where he lived. He insisted on pumping the water himself, all the while asking us about our trip and experiences.

By now, Dave and I had finished our first beers, a fact that did not go unnoticed by our new friends.

"Hey Bob, can't you see these guys are cyclists, get them another beer!" The bartender raced around and refilled our glasses.

"Has there been anything about our state that you haven't liked?" they wanted to know.

"The roads!" we said together.

137

The roads have been brutal. There are cracks in the pavement every ten yards or so. They aren't large cracks—most of the time they are no more than three to four inches across. If you are in a car, they probably have little effect. If you're on a bike, well, that's a whole different story.

One of our bar friends explained.

"The cracks allow for highway expansion. In the summer heat, the pavement expands, and the roads have room to breathe, In the winter the opposite occurs—the road contracts. The theory is that these cracks reduce overall maintenance costs."

Our glasses were again empty.

"More beer for the cyclists!"

"No, no, no!" Dave and I were emphatic—we had to get out of this bar and get to Dubuque. We reached for our wallets.

"Put that money away!

"No good in Iowa."

"We are the friendliest people!"

We laughed and thanked our friends. We walked out, adjusted our bodies to the heat, and continued on the road to Dubuque.

*   *   *

Ninety minutes later we were both in agony.

The stretch of road from the friendly bar to Dubuque was easily the roughest of the trip. I suppose I could do some fancy math and figure how many cracks we crossed, but it really doesn't matter. It seemed like three thousand.

Pop! Another jolt. Here comes another one—my body tightens in nervous anticipation. Pop! My whole body is jolted. This is a downhill run, but I am still braking because, Pop! I don't see how my, Pop! body will hold up over these, Pop! joints, or how my bike and, Pop! tires will survive.

Dave and I stopped at the first motel in Dubuque. The constant hammering damaged my nerves and muscles to the point where my fingers couldn't grip the pen to sign the registration form. My mental outlook wasn't much better. I sat in our room, and quietly considered the torture of the day.

Dave was quiet, too, but instead of reflecting, he was doing some productive thinking.

"Bill. I've got a great idea. We have a couple of options here in Dubuque.

"The heat, hills, and humidity are killing us. We need to get out of Iowa. One option is to board a riverboat. We could float on down to St. Louis or New Orleans, gamble, raise hell, rest our bodies, and then get back on our bikes and head east.

"Another option is to toss the Adventure Cycling maps, and strike out on our own. Instead of heading directly south to Davenport, as the maps suggest—and I figure that is another two days of brutal cycling—let's cross the Mississippi here and go into Illinois tomorrow."

The riverboat idea had great appeal, until we considered the ramifications. There are purists in the country that would put the dreaded asterisk by our names if we took a massive southern detour. I don't much care what purists think, but I sure don't want an asterisk next to my name. I know what that asterisk did to Roger Maris.

Bill Fitzpatrick* and Dave Fooshe* rode their bicycles across the United States of America.
Roger Maris** hit 61 home runs during the 1961 baseball season.

*   Of course, they travelled from Dubuque to New Orleans by riverboat.
**   Of course, it took him 162 games to do it.

In the morning, we agreed to head directly east from Dubuque, cross the Mississippi for the last time, and travel in a southeasterly path through Illinois.

Part Five

American Pride

Nothing much happened in Indiana. We're sure if you took the trip, though, it might be different. If you do, and something eventful does happen, please write to us. We'd like to know all the details.

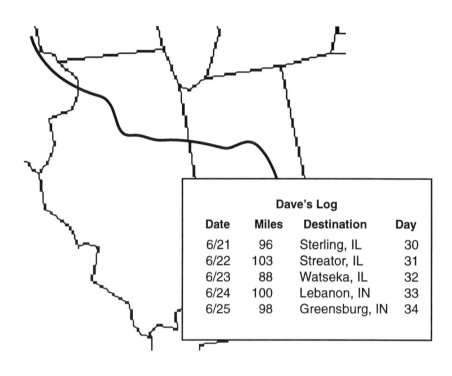

Dave's Log

Date	Miles	Destination	Day
6/21	96	Sterling, IL	30
6/22	103	Streator, IL	31
6/23	88	Watseka, IL	32
6/24	100	Lebanon, IN	33
6/25	98	Greensburg, IN	34

Scenery: ★★★

After you've seen one cornfield, you've seen them all.

Roads: ★★

In Illinois, there wasn't much traffic, but the country roads were exceptionally rough. In Indiana, there roads were marginally better, but the traffic was worse.

People: ★★★

"It's an average, Dave. Five for Illinois, one for Indiana. That comes out to a three.

Weather: ★★

I saw corn popping in the field. Honest, I wouldn't make anything up.

The Red, White & Blue

America! America!
God shed His grace on thee,
and crown thy good with brother–hood,
From sea to shining sea!

–Katherine Lee Bates,
America, the Beautiful

We have passed through many small towns during our journey, but none display as much American pride as those in Illinois.

Each one that we visit proudly displays the American flag. Not just one or two, either. Sometimes the entire business district is awash in the bright color of dozens of flags proudly fluttering in the warm midwestern air. These towns all have a definite Norman Rockwell flavor.

Dave and I stopped at the outskirts of Milledgeville, Illinois to stretch our legs and enjoy a snack. It was after 5:00 p.m., and we had a few more miles before we got to Sterling. We were on a county road that was surprisingly busy, considering we had seen little traffic during the day.

As the cars drove by, many of the people waved at us; not the wild "glad to see anybody" type waves we received in Montana and North Dakota, but more the index–finger–over–the–steering–wheel type waves. Their lingering looks reminded us that we were objects of curiosity with our tight–fitting bike shorts and brightly colored shirts.

A lot of the cars must have been on their way to a Little League baseball game. Dads were driving while their sons bounced up and down in the front seat. The boys in particular gave us long looks, their necks craning to see as they passed us in their cars.

What an American scene! A small midwestern town, the Stars and Stripes rippling in the wind, wheat fields in abundance, and dads taking their sons to the Friday night Little League baseball game.

I didn't grow up in the 1950's, but I guess these towns might remind many people of life during that period. I don't know for sure, but I suspect while the rest of our country has gone through war protests,

Watergate, Iran-Contra hearings, recessions, and the Gulf War, that not much has really changed in these small towns. The American flag is raised every day, work is done on the farm, church is on Sunday, and Little League games are held in the summer.

American Pride is alive and well in Illinois.

Dave & Gus

Gus Macker is proud to be the originator of the 3 on 3 basketball tournament that has taken Dr. James' original concept and transformed it into a game that everyone—regardless of size, shape, or age, can participate in and enjoy. So round up the kids and the dog, and join us for the ultimate celebration of basketball.

—Program from The Gus Macker Basketball Tournament

"It's time to get up Bill. Want bacon with your pancakes?"

"Sure," I mumbled. I had to pinch myself. Where am I? What's this, room service? I didn't recall ordering room service. And this sure is a nice motel room.

Only this isn't a motel room. Dave and I had slept comfortably in the beautiful home of Dave Lorenz, situated in the suburbs of Sterling, Illinois. Why are we here? Because of the Gus Macker basketball tournament.

Dave and I raced into Sterling yesterday afternoon—a gathering storm provided strong motivation. We arrived confident that we would find our standard small town motel and enjoy a nice hot dinner in a cozy restaurant. Large chilling rain drops splattered on our helmets as we took cover under the awning of an A&W Root Beer drive-in. Breathless from our five–mile sprint to find cover, we had barely beaten the downpour. This was not our preferred way to end the day. Still, we were dry, and a motel was, surely, just around the corner.

A fellow in his mid–twenties was sitting in his car enjoying the spectacle. We asked him for directions.

"No motel tonight, guys," Dave Lorenz replied as he finished his cheeseburger. "This is Gus Macker weekend. The motel rooms are all taken for at least fifty–miles."

I kicked the curb and swore because camping in the rain appeared to be our lot for the evening. I asked our helpful fellow for directions to the nearest campground.

"Well, I'm new to Sterling. Just moved here from Michigan. I don't know if there are any campgrounds or not. Tell you what, why don't you guys stay with me tonight? My wife and little girl are out of town so I have the whole house to myself. I would certainly welcome the company."

Dave and I were already on our bicycles, adjusting our chin straps. Yes, yes, yes. No campground for old Bill! We got directions, and started the short five–mile trek to his home. On the way, we stopped and purchased some groceries for dinner. Light rain continued to fall as we pulled into our host's driveway.

"So, tell us about this Gus Macker event," I asked Dave Lorenz. We were in his kitchen sipping on Heinekens and snacking on pretzels and black cherries. My old college roommate was whipping up spaghetti with all the extras, including mushrooms, green peppers, onions, and assorted spices.

"The Gus Macker is the biggest pick–up basketball tournament in the world," he explained. I eyed him suspiciously, so he continued. "Sterling and forty other cities across the country close down their streets, set up basketball goals, and let three man teams have at it. The players range in age from eight to eighty and a good portion of the entry fees are given to charity."

Holy Dr. Naismith! Where have I been? I've never even heard of this tournament. Dave Lorenz passed me the program.

Sure enough. In Sterling alone, almost three thousand players have entered the tournament. Ages six through seventeen make up half the field, ages eighteen through twenty–five a quarter of the field, with the other quarter above twenty–five years old. There are fifteen different states represented with the youngest player being six years old and the oldest a mere seventy–two. Females make up sixteen percent of the field. Last year, almost eighty thousand players participated, in front of seven–hundred thousand spectators.

While prizes and trophies are awarded, the Gus Macker seems less concerned with winners, as it is with having fun. The Gus Macker is definitely a red, white, and blue event. It is fitting that one of the tournament sites is in Illinois.

"Why did you ask us to stay at your house?" I asked Dave. So many people in the west and midwest have been extremely helpful. Strangers helping strangers, without questions or character references. This phenomenon has humbled me.

"You guys don't exactly look like criminals." Dave laughed. "People who do what you and Dave are attempting deserve support. I'm just glad that I can help out in this small way." As a weekend athlete and avid sports fan, Dave is fascinated with the whole idea of riding a bicycle across the country.

After dinner, I went upstairs to my private room. The rain beat against my bedroom window all night, and the wind gusts were severe. Nothing bothered me, though. I pulled up the blanket a bit higher and remembered the many kind people we have met. Out of nowhere, and for no apparent reason, many have offered us a helping hand.

Our host's pancakes were delicious. He kept them coming, too. He didn't stop to eat, but instead made sure that Dave and I had our fill. Our coffee cups were constantly refilled with the hot brew. For the first time, I missed the comforts of home. It would be nice to leisurely drink morning coffee, or sit on a couch and watch TV, or linger over the newspaper. We talked a while longer, and then said good–bye.

Dave and I stopped in town to watch a few minutes of the tournament. It wasn't hard finding the Gus Macker. Four or five blocks of downtown Sterling were already cordoned off for the event. The tournament was underway, with three man teams squaring off against each other in wild, frenzied activity. At least a thousand spectators were already enjoying the games.

Dave and I said good-bye to the Macker and the town of Sterling. It is another one of those dots on the map that we will not soon forget.

The Buda Boys

*"Exploring is delightful to look forward to and back
upon, but it is not comfortable at the time, unless it
be of such an easy nature, as to not deserve the name."*

—Samuel Butler,
Erewhon

During our last break of the day—we were just a few miles from
Streator, Illinois—I finally figured out why the midwest was so different,
and I was now ready to report the solution to Dave. Of course, he didn't
know I was working on the problem, so I had to start at the beginning.

"I got it, Dave. What I am about to tell you is so important that
you will want to write this down in your journal. Shall I wait for you to
get your pad and pen?"

Dave ignored me. Sometimes he doesn't react well to my frivolities.

"Very well. Then listen carefully. I am sure you will agree that
the midwest has been a comfortable and hospitable place for us to
cycle?"

"So?"

"And can you tell me why?"

"No."

"It's because everything is the same. We've met nothing but
white farmers and their friendly wives. I haven't seen a black person
since Stillwater. The last Indian sighting was back in northern Minnesota, and we certainly haven't seen any Hispanics or Mexicans. These
mid-westerners ought to be friendly and open. They haven't been sub-
jected to the stresses that have plagued other areas of the country. I
think many problems are caused by the geographic closeness of different cultures. Think of all of the unfortunate biases and mistrusts that
exist, and must co-exist, on a day-to-day basis. Not here in the midwest. Do you realize what I am saying? It's still the 1950's here! No civil
rights! No boat loads of refugees!

"Don't get me wrong, Dave. I am enjoying the kind and friendly midwestern people as much as you are. Wouldn't it be great if all places could be like this? I don't mean in a segregated way, of course, but with all races and nationalities co–existing, without all the strife." Here I started to wind down. This usually happens to me, my speeches are like slow leaky tires. They start out promising enough, but when the time is up, all the air is gone, and the pumps have to be brought in.

"Good point, Bill," my buddy said. He thought another half a minute, but no longer. He knows it takes a minute for me to get my major speeches re–inflated.

"I have a feeling that even if we were black orientals from Mexico we would be treated well in this part of the country," he said.

Black orientals from Mexico?

I got back on my bike and tried not to think about what Dave had just said.

*　　　　*　　　　*

Streator, Illinois, where we are staying tonight, is another one of the non-descript farm towns in central Illinois. Like the others we have passed, the town offers a couple of restaurants, a bank or two, and a small retail business district. From our point of view, there is not much to recommend the place other than it is only a day's ride back to Sterling and Dave Lorenz's comfortable home. We did, however, stop at one small town that left an impression.

Buda is located a mile or two off of a county highway. There is no restaurant in this small town, it only offers a grocery store and a few other small shops.

"More American flags than stores," I told Dave as we walked in to purchase our lunch at the grocery.

"Can I help you?" The speaker, a gentleman in his late fifties with thinning gray hair, was the store manager, and eager to help with our purchases. His wife, who looked a bit younger, ran the checkout counter.

"Just looking to pick up a few items for lunch," Dave said. "Any suggestions?"

"Since you boys have been cycling, you probably would like something hot. Got some cold ravioli here I can heat up in the micro-

149

wave, and some homemade chicken salad in the deli section. If you want to wash up, go on upstairs past our office, and you'll find our bathroom back there."

Dave and I did as he suggested, and headed to the checkout counter. His wife was helping another customer.

"Wait a minute," she told her. "I know you're in no hurry, let me help the cyclists. I know they're in a big hurry!" With that, she pushed aside her customer's purchases and checked us through. It was a phenomenon that Dave and I have often seen. Our unusual attire and unexpected presence seem to be the ticket to quick service. We told the nice lady that we were in no particular hurry, but still she hustled as if we were late for a wedding. After our groceries were rung up, we headed outside to eat our lunch. We soon had a couple of visitors.

*   *   *

"Impossible! No way!" exclaimed the small boy. "No one could do that! I tried to bicycle to my grandmother's last year, and I couldn't make it. I had to call my dad to come pick me up."

We were eating our lunch on the park bench outside the grocery store when two boys—no more than eight or nine years old—stopped riding their bicycles long enough to sit down and join us. We were talking about our epic journey when a third boy, a bit older, walked up and offered his experienced opinion.

"I don't believe anyone can ride a bicycle across the United States. That's just too far." His two friends, their mouths full of our chocolate chip cookies, looked on in wonderment as we explained.

"Sure you can," Dave started, "You just ride as far as you can every day for as long as it takes."

"But that's too hard," the older fellow responded, "why would anyone want to go that far?"

"Well, it's the best way I know to see the country first hand and up close," I offered.

"I don't believe you. Do you camp at night?"

I laughed and offered a weak, "Sometimes."

"Why don't you get a motorcycle? That would be easier."

"Yeah, and noisier, too." Dave was ready for that one.

"I still don't believe you. How many miles, so far?"

150

Dave checked his trusty cycle computer, "So far, we've been about twenty–five hundred miles. We've got about another twelve hundred to go."

"I'd never be able to do anything like that." The little boy's bravado was beginning to fade.

"Sure you could," replied Dave. "You can do anything you set your mind to, if you really want to."

"But, I could never do anything like that." he responded.

"I said the same thing when I was your age, and look at me now," Dave replied.

"Let's go play." With that, the three got on their bikes and left.

"Gee, Bill, do you think we might have had some impact on those kids?" Dave asked, somewhat discouraged that they had left so suddenly, as kids often do.

"Nope, the weasels just wanted our cookies. I'll go get us some more."

The Popsicle Gang

Through the ample open door of the peaceful country barn,
A sunlit pasture field with cattle and horses feeding.
And haze and vista, and the far horizon fading away.

—Walt Whitman,
A Farm Picture

"Hey, want a Popsicle?"

A small boy posed the question—he was perhaps eight or nine years old. We were so intent on our efforts to pedal another twenty miles, we had barely heard him.

"Sure," Dave said.

Seemed like a good time for one. Dave and I had been struggling all day. We were averaging twelve miles per hour, and taking breaks every hour. It was a day of hot headwinds in the Illinois farm country.

"Wait just a minute, I'll be right back," the boy said.

He ran back across the road, and entered the front door of a large two–story farmhouse. The lawn was meticulously groomed; I could easily envision stroking a few putts on it, or perhaps engaging in a game of croquet.

Our friend soon reappeared with two boxes of Popsicles, an over-sized notebook and four older brothers. They ranged in age from eight to eighteen, and were all neatly dressed and well behaved.

The Popsicle boy introduced himself and his brothers, "I'm Ernie Meister, and this is Paul, Peter, David and Evan. We've also got four sisters, but they're in town shopping today.

"Every summer, we give Popsicles to passing cyclists. We keep a record book. This year we've only seen about twenty other cyclists. Last year, we had a group of about fifty at one time. We almost ran out."

All of this was clearly documented—they showed us a large binder of notes and signatures from our predecessors. We proudly added our names and addresses.

152

"What are you going to be when you graduate?" I asked Paul, who appeared to be the oldest.

"I want to be a farmer." Paul said. "I'm going to college next year and I plan to study agriculture. We've got about eighteen hundred acres of land here. I like growing corn, wheat, alfalfa, soybeans and raising pigs and cattle. I like the Chicago Cubs, too."

"What about you?" I asked turning toward Ernie.

"I'm going to be a farmer, too," he replied.

"Me, too," replied Peter, David, Evan and Michael.

"Wouldn't you like to ride your bicycle across the country?" I asked Ernie.

"No way! I'd never do that," Ernie said emphatically. "Every time I ride my bike, the donkey chases me." With that, he pointed to the neatly trimmed gray donkey grazing inside the fence near the farmhouse.

We finished our Popsicles and thanked them for their kindness. I thought about giving the smaller boys a few quarters for their effort, but it didn't seem appropriate. These boys weren't doing it for the money.

Before we could pedal away, our friends insisted on refilling our water bottles with cold ice water. We followed them across the road to their outside pump.

"Not cold enough," yelled Paul. "Take it in to Mom!"

The small boys reappeared after a few minutes with our four bottles, packed with chipped ice and fresh water. Thanks didn't seem enough, but there wasn't much else we could say.

We pedaled a lot better after the Popsicles. I know a little about nutrition, so I'm not about to ascribe our improved pace to the cherry treats. I suspect just meeting and talking with the Popsicle Gang gave us the additional spirit needed to battle the winds.

*   *   *

Tomorrow, we will be in Indiana. Funny how impressions work. I always considered Illinois to be an urban area, with Chicago and its suburbs dominating the state. But my images of Illinois are now different. They are of American flags, and small town kindness. Of common sense, and hard work. Of small boys, with the desire to be farmers.

153

In an economic sense, Illinois, Montana and North Dakota should be similar. All are farming states, populated with people with a love for the land. There are differences, though.

The small Illinois towns are filled with optimism, and love of life, land and country. We haven't seen many visible signs of hardship. Most of the communities seem relatively vibrant. The people, too, are a happy lot. Optimism is in abundance.

The Montana and North Dakota towns are different. Melancholy grips the land and the people we met appeared to be in a constant struggle for survival. Perhaps this is to be expected. The harshness of the northern elements might even affect the outlook of Norman Vincent Peale.

Einstein, Golf and Band–Aids

There are only two questions that need to be answered in order to have a serene and Godly life. One could spend a life-time just meditating on these two questions and answers.

The first question is, "What time is it?"

The second question is, "Where are you?"

The only correct answer to the first is, "Now!"

The only correct answer to the second is, "Here!"

—William C. Martin,
The Way of the Word
(Reflections on the Art of Pastoring from Tao Te Ching)

Several years ago, I had the opportunity to visit the high school I had attended in Huntsville, Alabama. Nothing had changed at Grissom. The lockers were still painted orange. The hallway carpet was the same pea–green color that I remembered. It looked like it had not been changed since I graduated in 1972. The walls were still purple, green, yellow, and orange colors depending on which department you were in. And naturally, the institutional smell of the cafeteria hadn't changed.

I stopped for a few minutes in the physics lab. Still the same. I sat at my old desk, and felt as if I was eighteen again. What I remember most about physics were the lectures on Einstein, and his theories on time.

For the last two days, I have become preoccupied with the con-cept of time. Every hour or so I have pestered Dave—the keeper of the trip odometer—with "What's our average speed today?" or "How many miles have we covered?" It was not this way from Washington through Illinois. For almost four weeks, we cycled in rural oblivion. The time passed differently, moving as slowly and gently as the movement of wheat in a light summer breeze. Conversations with the local people were of equal pace, the words used were slow and thoughtful, and many times words weren't even necessary.

155

On our second day in Washington State, I turned off my bike odometer, because I didn't want to know the time and distance. These measurements are for people in an office, not for a person in search of a lost soul. I didn't want to be bothered with the daily news, that wasn't the point of the journey. If I bothered to buy a paper, it would be a local one, hopefully with less emphasis on the "crisis of the day" as reported by the national media. I also avoided television. The news would be the same when we returned. I wanted to focus on the "here" and the "now," and I was successful. Almost every day seemed unique and different, without the pressures of daily life. Without the relentless pursuit of profit and progress. Bookstores make millions of dollars on people looking for ways to get ahead.

"Seize the Moment?" On my desk at home. "The One Minute Manager?" Got that one, too. Like most, I am guilty of applying new Band-Aids with enthusiasm, without remembering that the adhesion is temporary, and bound to wash off in a few days. It's like a golf swing. You take a lesson, discover a cure, par a few holes, and then tell your friends it's all fixed. You may even give them a few unsolicited pointers. Naturally, bad things start to happen. Massive, majestic, slices come from the very clubs that had previously behaved like a Cub Scout at a White House reception. You sweat, and then you swear—first at your sticks, then at yourself, and finally, at your yapping buddies. You end up losing all the bets, and owe three foursomes multiple rounds of drinks on the club veranda. If you're lucky, the second round of drinks numb the pain, and you are free to go home and tell your wife it was a most successful day. You pour another drink, grab Golf Digest, and go on to the next Band–Aid. It will be there, we all know it.

Einstein's theories all relate to science, not to the human experience. Many religions and philosophies deal with the latter, however, and offer steadier directions, at least for me. But I must confess that while I know what I'm supposed to do, I often fail in the application. It is easy to sail away in the "here" and "now," when the "here" is Apgar, Montana, and the "now" is a bike trip on the backroads of America. It is not so easy when the adventures are over, and the winds start whipping up the waters.

*　　　　　*　　　　　*

When Dave and I left Illinois, things changed. The county road gave way to a trashy four–lane highway. Even though a nearby interstate carried most of the cars, the traffic was brisk. We did not expect this—we thought the transition to the east would be more gradual. We were wrong.

So far, there has been no relief in our trek across the state. Even the towns with promising names blur, their images no more remembered than if we were in a car racing at seventy miles per hour. The last two days, Dave and I have not been in the "here" and "now," instead we focus on the race to the next destination. What awaits us when we arrive? McDonald's and Burger King. The smell of car fumes, and the sounds of horns. Roads with no shoulders, and heavy urban traffic.

I think I need to work at forgetting the west. If I don't, well, it will take a long time to get to New Bern, North Carolina.

We Should've Camped

We two boys clinging together,
One the other never leaving,
Up and down the roads going,
North and South excursions making,
Power enjoying, elbows stretching, fingers clutching,
Arm'd and fearless, eating, drinking, sleeping, loving.
No law less than ourselves owning,
sailing, soldiering, thieving, threatening,
Misers, menials, priests alarming,
air breathing, water drinking,
on the turf or the sea beach dancing,
Cities wrenching, ease scorning,
statues mocking, feebleness chasing,
Fulfilling our foray.

—Walt Whitman,
We Two Boys Clinging Together

I suppose there might be several reasons—none of them good—why we said "No" to the attractive woman that invited us to follow her home for a glass of iced tea. It certainly wasn't the delivery of the invitation—she asked us with an engaging smile, and an enchanting accent. Her son—my guess is that he was seven or eight years old—stared at us from the back seat of the expensive blue and white van with wide-eyed curiosity, as if we were new playmates, whose bikes just happened to be a bit bigger than the one he owned. And Dave and I were thirsty from the days efforts. There had been no easy riding; we either cycled on rough, unmarked county roads—several times unsure that we were actually heading anywhere—or on the rough, narrow, trash-lined shoulders of the Indiana highways.

In fairness to Dave, I was the one that declined the invitation. My buddy was several car lengths ahead of me at a traffic light, and was oblivious to the kind offer. We had agreed to stop in the town of Rushville to get something cold to drink. After that, we planned to turn down Highway 3, towards the town of Greensburg.

"Sorry you can't make it," she said with a becoming smile. "Good luck with your trip." She had accepted, with equanimity, my feeble excuse that we "really have to be getting to Greensburg."

Like a moth drawn to light, I turned my attention to the map, and directed us out of town. Twenty miles and close to two hours later, we checked into a nondescript, sterile, "could be anywhere" motel, a safe ten minutes before six. Great! Made it on time! As Dave took his shower, I leaned my head on the pillow, and tried to rest, but it was useless.

On one level, this trip is about a reaching a goal. Dave, Ricky, and I had talked endlessly about our desire to cross the continent by bicycle. Which direction should we head? Should we go up to Canada? What about the possibility of crossing over the Great Lakes? What city should we start from? Where would we end? How many miles will it be? Do we have the time?

Were these the right questions to ask? Maybe not. I don't remember anyone saying, "Hey look, we will be going through Indian Reservations, let's bum around there for a while." Or better, "Forget the maps, let's just ride our bikes and see what we can find. If a place looks interesting, we'll stay there for a few extra days."

The bike maps we brought all encouraged the "goal–oriented" line of thought. There were even multiple routes to choose from. Why, we could follow that line through the central part of the country, or maybe drift through the northern part. The result was the same, however, we start on one coast, and end on the other.

Like most people, I like to think I am an independent thinker, and capable of free choice, but maybe that's not the case. All my life I've worked hard to be the best, to achieve, and to be successful. I've done that by focusing on a goal, deciding how to achieve the goal, and then executing the plan. And plain and simple, that is what's bothering me.

On another level, I took this bike trip to throw away the plans, to forget about goals and objectives, and do something unique and different. Schedules? Outta here! Responsibilities? A word I used to know! Deadlines? You got the wrong dude! In the western part of the country, both desires were fulfilled—my "goals and objectives" side, because we have, after all, cycled over two thousand miles without mishap, in relatively good time. And my "spiritual" needs were met, because it was an emotionally fulfilling time. Here in Indiana, though, I have this feeling that my spirit has been crushed—I did refuse the offer from kind lady in the van—and my "Type A" personality now dominates. My focus is on miles per hour, and reaching the next stop.

I guess if I want to look for reasons, there would be a couple I could use. Before leaving on the trip, I read John Steinbeck's book, *Travels with Charley*. It was an excellent account of his trip around the country, not by bicycle, but in a pickup truck he called Rocinante. His only companion was a French poodle named Charley. Steinbeck traveled the country, and spent time with many of the same type of people that Dave and I have encountered. What struck me was a comment he made, towards the end of the book, when he was in the southeastern part of the country. He said that he knew he was ready for the trip to be over. There were still a thousand miles ahead, and a week or two of travel, but he knew in his heart that the trip was over. No longer did he have the same keen interest, no longer did he make the extra effort to exit the highway, if only for a day or two. I now understand the meaning behind the words. It could be that after nearly three thousand miles, I too, am ready for the trip to be over.

Another possibility is my upbringing, and our culture. I've had the good fortune to travel the world, and meet many people from other countries. In contrast with much of the world, Americans have a desire to click off accomplishments, to set and meet goals, and to succeed in defined endeavors. People from other countries are different. They are more likely, for example, to take every last day of vacation, to spend the last dollar in pursuit of life, and to take trips down side roads. I've always envied this spirit, and tried to learn from it. I think it is good.

Maybe, in the end, we all desire to return to the life we leave behind. Back to the familiar, back to the routine of work and play, back to pressures and responsibilities.

It is also possible that we can absorb only so much at one sitting. Maybe I need a comfortable chair, a warm breeze, and time to consider the experiences of the trip.

*   *   *

Dave finally emerged from the shower. I came clean, and told him about the woman that invited us to her home for iced tea. He wasn't upset—but then again, I didn't tell him that she was pert, attractive, and downright sexy. Can't see any benefit in upsetting a man if you don't have to. After an average dinner, and quiet conversation, we both turned in for the night. We weren't asleep for long when...

Ka-doom! Whoommp! Ha! Ha! Ha! Ha!

At midnight, the room above us came alive. A loud raucous party was underway—complete with furniture tosses and body slams. I called the front desk and complained. All was quiet for fifteen minutes.

Ka-doom! Whoommp! Ha! Ha! Ha! Ha!

That was enough for me. I called the front desk and told them to expect a visit in the morning. At the appointed time, with little sleep between us, Dave and I approached the front desk. Before I could unleash my powerful well–rehearsed speech, the manager spoke.

"Don't worry about your bill. Wal–Mart will pick up the tab."

This didn't stop me from launching into my speech. "I want to let you know how miserable we were last night. We are cycling across the country, and stopped here because we wanted, well needed..." Then it hit me. He had already conceded a free room. "Well, yes, that's very nice, but what does Wal-Mart have do to with this?"

"The people in the room above you are trainees for Wal-Mart. Every now and then, they drink too much and get out of control, so Wal-Mart picks up the room tab. Last night, we called the police, and they hauled a few of them to jail."

While it was nice of Wal-Mart to pick up the bill, Dave and I would have gladly paid for a quiet night in another motel. Even a quiet campsite would have allowed more sleep.

The Valley of the Shadow

The mind is its own place, and in itself
Can make a Heav'n of Hell, a Hell of Heav'n.

—John Milton,
Paradise Lost

A mere thirty miles from the Ohio River and Kentucky, I mentioned to Dave that it might be nice to escape the traffic and narrow shoulders of the main highway for a while. He agreed.

We studied the Indiana highway map for a few minutes. It was easy identifying the Interstates and the main U.S. routes. The state roads, were also clearly marked. But the county roads? I suspect that Lewis and Clark would have problems deciphering the code.

The county roads were on the map—that was a plus. Unfortunately, there were no corresponding road signs. On the map they wandered across the land, like a beagle on the scent of a fat rabbit. They were colored in varying shades of gray, supposedly to assist the traveler in deciphering those roads that were paved, and those that weren't. Still, we thought, thirty miles? How much trouble can we get into?

We peered down a paved, unmarked road to our left. There were no signs or directions to indicate that the road actually went anywhere. An elderly lady, in her back yard gardening, told us that this was the road we wanted. After re-examining our maps, we headed into the Indiana wilderness.

At first, it was a pleasant change of pace. There were few cars, and the road wound around mountains, creeks, and valleys. Old crumbling stone walls added a certain charm to the landscape. Dave and I made one tough climb, and stopped for a break. We again examined our maps.

"Dave, I think we need to make a right turn at that abandoned grocery store. Do you see how it kind of matches the map?"

Dave studied the map with all of his engineering skill. He agreed with me, but not entirely. We looked around to see if anyone could provide assistance, but the area was deserted.

We decided to turn right. To validate our thinking, a large truck loaded with construction material went racing by. He must be going to Veevay. Near this city was the bridge that would carry us over the Ohio River into Kentucky.

After a short climb, we crested a ridge and headed back down the mountain. It was a long glorious descent, complete with winding turns and scenic views. Little did we know that this road was leading us to the Valley of the Shadow of Death. This part of the road was window dressing; it was the apple from the Garden of Eden, and we munched hungrily. We were looking for more apples when...

Sccrcccchhh!

Dave and I slammed on our brakes. We rounded a turn and discovered that our apple was wormy. The paved road ended and we skidded onto gravel. It was difficult to tell, however, where the gravel might end. The thick forest blocked our view, and the road turned and twisted like a coiled snake.

Dave and I considered our options. It was a long two mile climb back to the top of the mountain, with no guarantee that we weren't on the right road all along. After all, we had seen a big truck come this way. We made the decision to continue down the mountain. Loose gravel made the descent treacherous. We had all the traction of a hog on ice.

Our descent into the underworld continued. Occasionally, we saw meager signs of life such as a run–down shack, or trailer. These dwellings, tucked behind the trees and brush, were not places you would expect to find a kind, helping hand. No milk and cookies at these places. More like moonshine.

Dave and I skidded around a corner, and jammed on the brakes. Yes, we were at the bottom. An old covered bridge, colored with faded red paint, crossed a small dark creek. We traversed it gingerly, not wanting to awaken the demons that surely slept underneath.

How did we ever manage to find ourselves in this neighborhood? I imagined evil lurking behind every tree. Burned–out shells of deserted automobiles lined the old gravel road. Did I hear banjos from the movie *Deliverance*?

An old woman with scraggly gray hair swerved past us on the bridge in her beat–up black Volkswagen. She didn't wave, smile, or slow down. We could be murdered out here and no one would ever know.

"Nice place, huh, Bill?" Dave's comment jolted me from my downward spiral of fear and depression.

"Yeah, Dave."

Still pedaling on gravel, we soon began our climb out of the valley. We were forced to walk our bikes up most of the grades, since our tires spun fruitlessly in the loose gravel. Where was this road leading? It was, by now, a narrow, one lane path.

At last, we crested a hill and placed our tires on firm cement. Simultaneously, the sun reappeared, or did I only imagine that it had ever left? Nice homes with fenced in yards were a welcome sight. We stopped and got directions from the first farmer we found. We were still twenty–five miles from Veevay, but happy to be out of the Valley of the Shadow.

*   *   *

Once out of the valley, it took us another two hours to reach the town of Veevay. In mid–afternoon, we crossed into Kentucky, got on Highway 455, and set our sights on the town of Dry Ridge.

Part Six

Take Me Home Country Roads

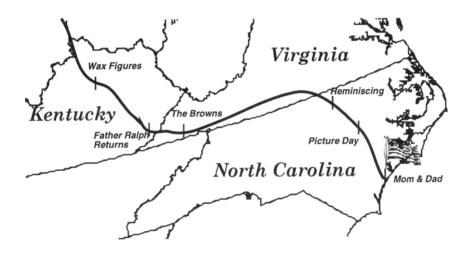

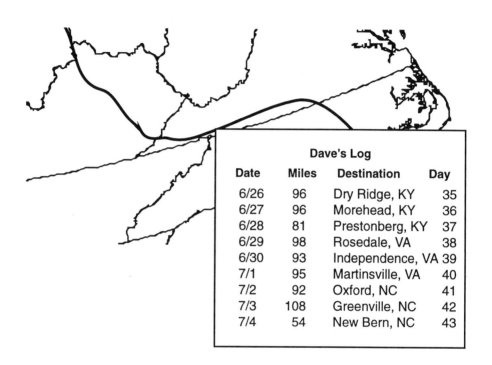

Dave's Log

Date	Miles	Destination	Day
6/26	96	Dry Ridge, KY	35
6/27	96	Morehead, KY	36
6/28	81	Prestonberg, KY	37
6/29	98	Rosedale, VA	38
6/30	93	Independence, VA	39
7/1	95	Martinsville, VA	40
7/2	92	Oxford, NC	41
7/3	108	Greenville, NC	42
7/4	54	New Bern, NC	43

Scenery: ★★★

The Appalachian Mountains are difficult to cycle, but if you can overlook the overwhelming poverty, it is beautiful country.

Roads: ★

Coal chunks on the highway, narrow winding roads, and the occasional redneck made the touring less than enjoyable.

People: ★

"I'm not passing moral judgement, Dave, I'm just saying the people in Kentucky didn't feel like talking to us."

Weather: ★

Miserable heat.

Welcome to Kentucky

Everybody's talkin' at me
I don't hear a word they're sayin'
Only the echoes of my mind.

People stoppin' starin'
I can't see the faces
Only the shadows of their eyes.

—Fred Neil,
Everybody's Talkin'

When we crossed into Kentucky from Indiana, we noticed several profound changes.

Although we are only a hundred miles from Cincinnati, familiar southern accents greet us for the first time.

Hopeless poverty is apparent. Withered shacks, rusted trailers, abandoned automobiles, and garbage now litter the landscape. This is easier to handle than the mental poverty. Even in the more prosperous neighborhoods, our greetings are met with suspicion.

The books I have read about other cyclists that have pedaled through Kentucky all mention that this is a lousy state for touring. Maybe it is a self–fulfilling prophecy, but, so far, I have to agree.

*　　　　*　　　　*

"We'd like a room for the night."

I addressed the question to the five adults sitting in the lobby of the "Motel" motel in Dry Ridge Kentucky. It was a plain lobby, with a few vinyl chairs, one fake plant, and a weathered tile floor. The five looked at us and did not say a word. An older woman got up, and walked behind the counter.

"Thirty–two dollars," she replied solemnly.

"Yes ma'am," I responded. "That will be fine." The other people in the lobby stared straight ahead, refusing to acknowledge our presence.

"Sure glad you have a room," I said, "we're bicycling across the country, and after a hundred miles today, we're looking forward to a nice hot shower."

I might have added, "And we're already fed up with the great state of Kentucky. After twenty–five hundred miles of friendly people, we have yet to receive as much as a smile in this state."

Brought up to be polite, however, I didn't say that.

"It was hot today," she offered meagerly, dispensing her goodwill from an eye dropper. The four other people continued to looked straight ahead, as if they were intent on winning the coveted "Most Likely to be Mistaken for a Wax Figure" team award.

"Yes ma'am, sure was," I ventured. Nothing else was said. I took the room key and left.

*　　　*　　　*

After several minor disasters, Dave and I began to compile a list of "Rules of the Road." A few of these are important enough to mention.

- If you don't know where you are going, don't lead the way.
- Don't ever camp.
- Never change a tire in a swamp.
- Take plenty of money on a trip like this. You'll end up eating it.
- Never stay in a motel named "Motel."

"Whew," Dave said, "'til today, the people we've met have been friendly, outgoing, and at least mildly curious about our journey. We check in at 'Motel' motel, and, even though five adults are in the lobby, just sitting around, no one says a word. No one asks where we're from. No one asks where we're headed. Not that it matters, but no one seems to care about two skinny strangers in funny pants that just pedaled up on their bicycles."

"You'll feel better after a cold beer," I told Dave. "I'll buy."

While Dave showered, I hiked back up the busy highway to a small grocery we had passed on the way in, and headed back to the cooler. Nothing. No beer. Tired, thirsty, and dragging, I went back up to the cashier and pleaded, "Where's the beer?"

"Sorry, Drah Redge is in a drah cownty, ya'll ahafta gowan up the enter staight 'bout fiftain mailes to the next cownty fer beher."

"I rode my bicycle a hundred miles today, and I want a cold beer!"

The people in the checkout line laughed, as if I was attempting to order Coquille St. Jacques at McDonalds. When I got back to the room, though, Dave was not amused. I listened to his ranting and raving about choice and free enterprise as we walked over to the Country Grill restaurant. We enjoyed a very nice dinner of catfish with blueberry pie for dessert, and while it would be nice to say I felt marginally better about Kentucky, it would not be true at all.

*   *   *

Our plan tomorrow is to burrow deeper into the hills of Kentucky. We will stay on Highway 36, and perhaps make it as far as Morehead, a distance a of about a hundred miles.

A Tale of Two Cities

And in the naked light I saw,
Ten thousand people, maybe more,
People talking without speaking,
People hearing without listening,
People writing songs, that voices
never share, no one dare,
Disturb the sounds of silence.

—Paul Simon,
The Sounds of Silence

I felt as if we were on the set of a *Twilight Zone* episode. I could hear Rod Serling's voice intoning the introduction to the episode:

"Bill Fitzpatrick and Dave Fooshe. Two men who thought they were on a mission. Two men who thought they were heading to the North Carolina coast. Little do they know that they have been pedaling to a different kind of place. A place where their accomplishment will not be recognized. A place where they will be invisible. They will be in the dark deep recesses of—*pause*—Cynthiana, Kentucky."

No one gave us even the slightest notice.

Poverty didn't appear to be an excuse, either. Dave and I were sitting on a park bench directly across the street from the well–kept courthouse. Our bikes rested comfortably against the red brick building of a multi-partner law firm. Most of the buildings on Main Street were neat and tidy, but if this town had a T–shirt, it would read "Not Interested."

Businessmen in suits hustled by without a glance. Lawyers popped in and out of their offices and paid us little attention. Housewives darted by too, their eyes seemingly focused on a small piece of the sidewalk. I glanced at the sidewalk just to make sure I wasn't missing a big spider, a pack of rats, or a dead bat. Nope, nothing.

Dave and I sat on the bench eating lunch for close to an hour. Finally, an elderly gentleman came by, stopped to say hello, and offered directions out of town. They could see us! Our visitor had a deep drawl which was difficult to understand. Dave, having lived in California too long, had no clue to what was being said. I got about half the words.

We packed up our groceries, and left as quickly as we could. There was no reason to linger in Cynthiana.

*   *   *

The town of Carlisle is only fifteen miles from Cynthiana. As we walked into a Dairy Queen for a yogurt, I girded myself for the same indifference we had encountered in Cynthiana.

"How are you guys doing? Tell me about your trip." A very attractive young lady at the Dairy Queen was interested in our journey. While we chatted, two other folks joined in the discussion. After finishing our yogurt, we pedaled into town to buy some Gatorade. I rested outside the grocery store while Dave made the purchases.

"Hi. Are you having fun?" Two elderly ladies came up to me and quizzed me about the trip. "Well, yes," I responded. I blinked my eyes. This town was sure different than Cynthiana.

A teenager came by and stopped to chat.

"Where y'all headed?" he asked.

We told him of our adventure. His excitement was evident.

"My dad owns the grocery store, and I know he will want to talk to you. He runs marathons, and has always talked about riding a bicycle across the country. Will you wait here while I go get him?"

We told him we would wait, and in a few minutes his dad came out to talk.

"Yes, I have run the marathon. My favorite is the Boston Marathon—I've done that one several times. I try to stay in shape, but as you can see, I've not been able to do much lately. I broke my leg several months ago in an accident around the house. In a few more weeks I'll be able to take the cast off, and hopefully, start running again. Which way you guys headed anyway?"

I told him we were headed towards Morehead.

"Watch out for wild dogs," he advised. "There are some mean ones out there. One has bitten me seven or eight times—I finally started carrying a stick."

"Bitten by the same dog seven or eight times?" I said. "What are you waiting for? Waste him!"

That's what I was thinking. What I said was, "I hope that dog doesn't get me. I can't believe your bad luck."

Dogs are now one of Dave's favorite topics. "We have pedaled three quarters of the way across the country, and had not been chased by a single dog until we arrived in Kentucky. I think a dozen came after us today. Even the chemical sprays we brought didn't help much. I had a direct hit on one dog today, and while that did slow him down, I didn't see his two friends until it was almost too late. I went berserk, and unloaded the whole can."

The dogs have been scary. There is nothing like the full throttled snarl of a large German shepherd to motivate the naked cyclist. They come from all directions, too, usually with no advance warning.

"Why here?" Dave asked our friend. "Kentucky is the poorest state we've been in. What are people doing with these wild dogs?"

Our marathon man provided an answer. "People who keep vicious dogs usually have something to hide."

While talking to our friend, several other people came up to say hello. Hard to believe this friendly town of Carlisle is only fifteen miles from—*pause*— Cynthiana.

*   *   *

We got back on our bikes and continued down Highway 36. The first few miles from Carlisle were pleasant enough—our path took us along swift moving creeks and productive farmland. Traffic was scarce, so Dave and I enjoyed a pleasant mid–afternoon ride.

It was to change, however. As we approached the Daniel Boone National Forest, we again saw the dark side of Kentucky.

That Old Kentucky Home

Listen, here the sound, the child awakes.
Wonder all around, the child awakes.
Now, in his life, he never must be lost,
No thought must deceive him, in life he must trust.

—John Lodge, Moody Blues
Eyes of a Child

It was like one of the many other rotting buildings I have seen during the trip. A hundred yards further up the hill, and a hundred yards closer to the shack, I changed my mind. It wasn't like the other ones at all. This was different.

In size, it wasn't much larger than a child's play house, the type you see in the backyard of a well–manicured suburban home. A tall adult, one over six foot two or three, would certainly have to stoop to enter, or else risk a sharp blow to the forehead. Negotiating the porch to even get to the front door would be a challenge. I guessed that for every two plank boards in place, there was a missing one, the gaps as evident as missing keys on a piano. Was this someone's home?

Chickens, roosters, and a couple of small pigs wandered about in front of the shack, careful to avoid the tires, hubcaps, sinks, and other trash littering the area. It is safe to assume these animals were permanent, well-satisfied tenants, for there was not even a fence to keep them from wandering off.

I suppose if I had only seen the man of the house, the scene might not have been so troubling. It was the children I won't forget. Two little girls, wearing limp, faded blue dresses, walked out of the front door, and wandered around the yard, their bare feet sharing the same brown dirt used by the animals. An older woman, I can only suppose it was their mother, also came out, and sat down on the porch. At first, she watched only the girls, but then her attention was diverted to two cyclists, each dressed in snappy biking attire. I'm guessing, but I suspect she also noted the miniature American flags that each cyclist had in their rear panniers. Whatever feelings she might have had, she kept to herself, for she then turned her attention back to the children. One of the cyclists thought about the girls. Who reads them stories? Who gives them hope? Why didn't I wave?

*   *   *

Dave had been expanding on his Corridor Theory for the better part of the trip. Always an optimist, I generally agree with Dave's thoughts on opportunities and outlooks. But what about Kentucky? What hope exists for these people?

Dave made the attempt, "I still think there is a corridor of hope for the poor people in Kentucky. But what I think doesn't matter. These people have to think there is hope or nothing will change.

"As for that family today, I feel sorry for their condition, but I wonder how they view it? Maybe that is all they know and expect. Have you ever noticed how large outcomes often turn on very small events or decisions? A child decides to obey his parents rather than be rebellious. A teenager decides not to join his friends in smoking and drinking. A high school student graduates, even though his friends are all dropping out. Small decisions, but all with potentially tremendous outcomes.

"This may sound callous, but I expect these folks' current condition is a result of their attitudes. How can you turn things around if you don't believe that hard work and positive attitudes make a difference?"

I blinked. What had gotten Dave started down this path?

"So tell me, Marley, what chance hath they to dream of a brighter Christmas future?" I teased, attempting to lighten the mood with my best Dickensian accent.

"Education is the key, but not the type of education offered by the public school system and the big government programs. These people need to be taught simple things like how to learn. They need to learn why a positive outlook is important. I suppose we learned these things at home and in church, but like many, took them for granted. Today we've seen both sides. The folks in Cynthiana didn't give us the time of day, yet fifteen miles away, in Carlisle, the local residents were friendly and outgoing. And in between, we saw those poor people whose lives might have been different had they only been aware of the Corridor Theory."

Caudill

Depend not on another, but lean instead on thyself...
True happiness is born of self reliance.

—The Laws of Manu

Thirty miles from Prestonberg, Dave and I stopped for an afternoon Gatorade. For one of the few times in this state, someone came up and asked us about our trip.

"How far have ya'll ridden?" asked Caudill. Caudill is a forest ranger for a nearby state park. He is also an avid cyclist.

Dave and I were thrilled to find someone, anyone, in Kentucky who was interested in our trip. We spent at least thirty minutes answering all of his questions. Caudill appeared to be in no hurry to leave.

Sccrrchhh!

An automobile well past its prime skidded into the parking lot. The occupants were perfectly suited to the car. In the front seat were a man and woman, and there was another woman in the back. They all appeared to be in their forties. He was wearing what used to be a white T–shirt and cut–offs. Both women wore tank tops and cut–offs. Among the three of them, I counted twelve teeth. All of those were in the front seat.

Caudill knew these people and he gave them a friendly wave.

But a wave wasn't enough for the woman in the back with no teeth.

"Hey Caudill, why don't y'all come on overta mah playce tonight?" she hollered, "I'll showya a good time!"

Caudill smiled and shook his head at the woman in a good natured way. That didn't stop the woman from screaming some more.

"Lookit you. Sittin' undera tree, drinkin' Gatorade, and wastin' taxpaiyer's munee! They oughter lock you up!"

The more she screamed, the less I understood. At last they tired of their sport and drove away. We asked Caudill about the woman in the back.

"Aw, she don't mean no harm. You wouldn't want to mess with her, though. She's been married five times, and been in other trouble besides. She's really got no place to talk about wasting taxpayer's money—she's spent some time in jail, too. She's the kind of person you should try to avoid."

We assured Caudill we had no intention of crossing the toothless woman. Dave and I had been on the road a long time, but not that long. The "authentic" Mexican food we had for dinner in Morehead last night was bad enough, we didn't need any more trouble.

Over the past several years, Caudill has voluntarily gone out west to work on forest fires and other special projects. Dave mentioned the burned areas we had seen on our ride up Sherman Pass. It turns out that Caudill had been there. He said it was the biggest forest fire he'd ever seen, and it took weeks to put it out.

Caudill, although shy and soft spoken, was enthusiastic about bicycling and quite in awe of our accomplishment. He talked of his experiences cycling in the area.

"I really like cycling a lot, but you have to take a lot of heat from the local boys about the sport, and the clothing. I suppose they don't see the challenge of it. But I really like it."

Caudill didn't seem the type to get too upset about what other people thought. My kind of guy.

*   *   *

I don't often ask people personal questions when I first meet them. On this trip, however, I have been a bit more aggressive. After all, you have but a few minutes in these chance encounters to learn more about each other, so why hold back? I think the other person also recognizes this, and is more likely to "open up." Still, my question to Caudill wasn't really that personal, it was his response that was interesting. It provided a glimpse of what life in the Appalachians was once like.

"Is Caudill a family name?" I asked.

"Not quite," he laughed. "I'm known in this part of the country as a 'Caudill Baby.' I figure there are about fifty of us in this part of Kentucky that are named Caudill.

"You see, back when I was born in 1953, there weren't a whole lot of doctors in the area. We had to depend on just a couple of 'em to deliver all of the babies, fix all the broken bones and stuff, and look after all of the people with long term illnesses. These doctors didn't ever really keep office hours, because many of their patients didn't have the money or means to travel to see them. So these traveling doctors become known to everybody.

"Well, one of these country doctors, a woman named Dr. Claire Louise Caudill, delivered me. That's where my name comes from. I guess there are several dozen of us named 'Caudill' in the state. 'Course, there are lots of children named Louise or Claire in the area as well. By the time she retired ten years ago, she figured she had delivered over eight thousand babies. She always made the trip too, it didn't matter how cold, snowy, or wet things were. She'd show up, stay as long as necessary, and then go on to the next house. She never refused to help either. No sir. Just because someone didn't have much cash, or might still owe from the last call, was no reason for Dr. Caudill to refuse their need. People would give her what they could, when they could. Sometimes it might be some fresh vegetables, all canned up. I heard that some former patients would give her home-made flannel pajamas, so that if they needed her on a cold winter night, all she'd have to do is pull on a pair of old jeans.

"Now I said she retired, but I really didn't think that's quite right. I hear she still lives up near Morehead, and still works a few days a week. That amazing, isn't it? I figure she must be over eighty years old now. You know, I don't remember if The Waltons had a doctor in their show, but if they did, I'm sure he or she was a lot like our Dr. Caudill.

*   *   *

Following Caudill's directions, we arrived in Prestonberg around 6:00 p.m. After checking into a Super 8 Motel, we ordered a double-cheese pizza and plotted our escape from Kentucky.

The Breaks

Strip mining, while it is going on, looks like the devil, but...
if you look at what these mountains were doing before this stripping,
they were just growing trees that were not even being harvested.

—Aubrey J. Wagner, TVA Chairman (1960's)

This morning, Dave and I left Prestonberg, Kentucky and crossed into Virginia. It was a rough ride. The narrow roads and heavy traffic made our experience less than enjoyable. It was necessary, too, to keep a careful eye out for the large chunks of coal that litter the roads. We are deep in Appalachian coal country. Our first stop was at a grocery store in Elkhorn City to pick up food for lunch.

During our stop, an older, well–dressed gentleman walked over and asked, "Y'all headinta Virginny?"

"Yes, sir," Dave responded, "we are going to Honaker today."

"On them bikes? No way!" he exclaimed. "It's too fer and the country's too rugged. Y'all awta camp fer the night at The Breaks Interstate Park. It's only fiftain miles er so from here, and it's beeuutyfull. We call it the "Grand Canyun of the East.""

"Sounds great," said Dave, "but we need to make it to Honaker."

"No, y'all need to camp at The Breaks!" This guy was insistent. "Y'all ul never make it ta Honaker."

Dave shrugged his shoulders. We have both heard "You'll never make it" from well–meaning people before.

Dave and I left Elkhorn City and completed the difficult climb up to The Breaks. It is a beautiful park—the gentleman had not lied—water has cut deep canyons in the mountains, making the view from the summit truly stunning. We rested for a while and savored the view. We were running low on water, so Dave started down a nearby trail to look for a fountain.

As I gazed into the mist that guarded the distant mountains and valleys, I wondered about that which I could see, and that which I couldn't. That's when I heard the familiar voice.

"Hello, Bill, enjoying your trip?"

178

He was back. I turned to see his stately outline perched on a rock near the edge of the cliff. I knew he wouldn't wait for the finish line. Priests don't stay away for long.

"My son, it's me, Father Ralph."

"Hi, Father. What are you doing here?" I said. "But, it's good seeing you," I quickly added. I didn't want him to get the idea he wasn't welcome.

"I've come to talk to you, my son. You've not been fair to the people of Kentucky, and I feel that you need some guidance."

I sagged. Same old Father Ralph. I wish this guy would leave me alone.

"My son, I was pleased with your balanced accounts of the many difficult Indian issues in the west. You made an effort to understand the people and the land. You toured the area with an open mind, and asked many questions. You did not do that in Kentucky."

I made a feeble attempt to explain my feelings.

"Father Ralph, first of all, the people in this part of the country won't talk to you, so how can I know about their feelings? Secondly, I'm only trying to report my impressions. After all, Father Ralph, this is a bike trip, not a sociology project."

That's telling Father Ralph! Maybe he will go away.

"My son, you didn't bother to ask the 'why' questions. You are guilty of arrogance and righteousness."

Maybe we were at the penance step. I took the plunge.

"OK, Father Ralph. I'll say three Hail Mary's, an Our Father, and donate some money to your new school." This was one of his favorite projects. Maybe I could buy my way out of this mess.

"No, my son. Your penance is to listen to the story of these poor children—some told in their own words."

I looked around. Dave was still gone. There was no place to run and no place to hide. I agreed to listen.

Father Ralph began, "Like most of America, Kentucky has not always been as you see her today. Listen to the voices of those who knew a better time."

"When I went out to teach in 1926 there were hundreds of roadless creek valleys all through the Southern Appalachians, and almost no roads at all in Eastern Kentucky...

...The best homes were usually the older log houses, and around those log houses there were many pleasant things including much that was beautiful; for those who like open fires, children, human talk and song instead of TV and radio, the wisdom of the old who had seen all life from birth to death, none of it hidden behind institutional walls, there was a richness of human life and dignity seldom found in the United States today"

—Harriette Simpson Arnow, Author

"I celebrate the fact that this Appalachia has a hold on me. Wherever I go, I'm of these hills. That little cabin at the head of the holler has been in the back of my mind, like an anchor with a long rope, all the time I've been having to make a home for my family elsewhere—and someday soon I mean to build that cabin, because here is where I belong. No one has to tell me that—I know."

—Jean Ritchie, Songwriter

Father Ralph continued, "And listen to those who knew her during the period of change."

"This is the day of the giant bulldozer, the hideous grinding auger, machinery of the strip miner, and the smoke and dust of them hang over the ridges and hollers of eastern Kentucky like a pall of sorrow. This is the time when all of the sins of the previous generations caught up with us.

For my Grandpa Hall, it was an unwitting sin. He, along with most of his neighbors, sold the mineral rights to his land to the friendly, likable man who said he represented a company that thought there might be a little coal on our land worth getting out. The company was willing to take a big chance and pay Grandpa 50 cents an acre, and since Grandpa had more than a thousand acres, this amounted to *around $500. 00, a handsome sum in those days. For a man with a dozen children, it was also impossible to refuse."*

—Jean Ritchie

"It's really hard to believe that eighty-some years ago, the husband and wife who signed that deed with an 'X' could really envision what the results of their actions would be."

—J. T. Begley, Attorney

"Strip mining began on a large scale around 1961 in East Kentucky. By 1964 large areas of Pike, Knott, Harlan and Lechter Counties had been gutted...

...As months passed it became clear that the only farms saved from strip mining were places where small landowners, family and friends, were willing to physically stop the stripping machines. Almost without exception the courts backed the coal companies, not the small landowners."

—Mike Clark, Past Appalachian Program Director

"This is (strip mining), the cheapest kind of mining, but it does the most damage. Reduced to essentials, it consists of blasting and bull-dozing the top off a mountain to expose the coal seam that lies beneath, and then loading the coal into trucks and carting it away. The relocated mountain top winds up, by force of gravity, in the valleys below. After a heavy rain, it becomes mud and moves like lava until it reaches the bottom of the valley, where it slides into streams, becomes silt, and is washed through the tributaries of eastern Kentucky into the Kentucky River, and then the Ohio, and the Mississippi, and finally into the Gulf of Mexico—where a great deal of eastern Kentucky lies today."

— Thomas N. Bethell, Writer–Photographer

Father Ralph said, "And now listen to those who suffered."

"We was bein' told to do whatever the company and bosses told us to do, regardless of what hardships it was—goin' in water holes and standin' in water to our knees to load coal.

I've come home many a night in the wintertime, way after dark, come in with my clothes froze so stiff they would stand up. They'd done eat supper and all gone to bed and my old mother'd hear me go by and she'd say, 'There's poor little Jim—listen to his clothes rub together, froze stiff.' If you'd forget and pull your cap off too quick, it would pull your hair out—be frozen to your hair.

It was just a way of making people be slaves, because they had to do that to live.

But we done it, didn't we, brother Jake?"

—Jim Hamilton, Disabled Coal Miner

*   *   *

Father Ralph continued, "Most of the voices I've shared with you, my son, are the voices of people from twenty to thirty years ago. As with the Indians, the wrongs of previous generations are not easily forgotten or corrected. There is still a suspicion of outsiders—a suspicion that will linger for generations."

Father Ralph Returns

As the time draws nigh glooming a cloud,
A dread beyond of I know not what darkens me.

I shall go forth, I shall traverse the States awhile,
but I cannot tell whither or how long,
Perhaps soon one day or night while I am singing
my voice will suddenly cease.

O book, O chants! must all then amount to but this?
Must we barely arrive at this beginning of us?
—and yet it is enough, O soul;
O soul, we have positively appear'd—that is enough.

—Walt Whitman,
As the Time Draws Nigh

"Come on Father Ralph, let's ride together for a few miles."

I sensed from Father Ralph's last conversation that he was getting impatient with me. That wouldn't do at all—no reasonable person wants a priest to be angry at them. I figured it was time for an honest discussion.

"I've been waiting for you to ask me," he replied, "I'll go change."

With that, Father Ralph disappeared into the bushes, changed his clothes, and in less than five minutes, reappeared with a black, slightly used Cannondale touring bike.

"Haven't done this in years," he said. "That's one reason I volunteered for your journey. Besides, it got me off confession duty for six straight weeks. Sometimes I get a bit down, sitting in that dark closet, listening to people confess the same sins again and again. Had Dan Rather in last week."

"Er, what was on his mind?" I asked cautiously. I thought maybe in a "big picture, overview" sense, he could kind of let me know if we were dealing with a mortal sin or a venial sin—I didn't need to know all the details.

"Nope, can't tell you," said Father Ralph. With that, he mounted his bike, and pedaled smartly down Highway 80. I hustled to catch him.

"Father, why have you bothered, I mean visited me, during this journey?"

"It's the rule, my son. Whenever a person mentions that they want to go look for their soul, one of us is assigned the responsibility of assisting in the search. We take all requests seriously, even when they come to us in a smart–ass sort of way."

Before he continued, he gave me one of his withering looks.

"I visited you at that shabby bar in Montana because you had lost sight of the purpose of your journey. You were so immersed in the adventure of it all, that you forgot to learn, and understand, the lessons that were being presented. After I left, you remembered for a while, but when you hit the big cities—you forgot again. Frankly, you teed me off, so I left you in Iowa, and sent Sister Katherine to visit you. I think she caught up with you at a small restaurant in Harper's Ferry.

Ha! I knew it! That wasn't even an agricultural reporter Dave and I were talking to way back in Iowa. It was a Nun, posing first as a reporter, and then as an agricultural reporter, that was spying on us. The last time I felt this snookered was on a date with an adamant feminist. I thought I understood the whole concept of the woman's movement until the sizable dinner check was presented. Waiter! Waiter! Where's my date?

"Then, my son, I decided to send you through Kentucky, to put you through some of the poorest parts of your country. I hoped that the experience might create an awareness, or perhaps even a sense of responsibility, for those that are less fortunate than you. But, no, you raced blithely through the state, condemning and not understanding, answering and not questioning, and forgetting, that by the grace of God, well, you know the rest. What is it with your generation? Do you think it's all Club Med vacations and Aspen ski trips? That baggage doesn't make one happy."

Of course, the priest was right. Some of the happiest people I've met have never skied the back bowls of Vail. Some of the saddest people I've met have. Perhaps it was time to ask Father Ralph for direction.

"So where is my lost soul, Father Ralph?" I asked, seriously. "Do you think it's a few more miles down the road?"

Father Ralph understood my metaphor. "Yes, my son. You must understand that, while on earth, your conscience is your soul. Unfortunately, only at times of great stress do people call on this spiritual reserve to help them through a crisis. However, if the soul has not been exercised and developed, it will be unable to support the questioning non–believer. What you need to do, is to consistently remind yourself of your blessings, the love God has for you and your family, and to live each day with peace, understanding, and compassion. When you learn to do that, you will have found your soul."

I considered Father Ralph's words. Dave and I have certainly touched the soul of the land; I would think it impossible to take the journey we have, and not feel the spiritual element of the Cascades and Rockies, the plains and farmland, and yes, even the sad state of Kentucky. We have also felt the hunger of many people—mostly all yearning to take the same trip, to get away from the daily grind, and at least in a symbolic sense, take a bike trip. Dave and I are fortunate to have been the participants—we have touched and seen the unrealized desires and broken dreams of many observers. But Father Ralph is right—I will not find my soul on a bike trip. Finding a soul is a lifetime of work. Journeys start with small steps, and with Father Ralph's assistance and companionship, perhaps even I can travel the road.

"Don't worry my son, just do your best. There aren't too many people that truly find their souls on earth." Father Ralph attempted to console me—I think he could tell I was disappointed. Finding my soul was not going to be easy. I was already thinking about the ways I'd have to change. For starters, I'd have to alter the way I look at the world. Yuppie baiting—out! Democrat bashing—gone the way of the martini! All stereotypes—shot to, well, whatever! What would I have left to talk about?

As if reading my mind, the wise priest gave me one last piece of advice. "There's nothing wrong with having a laugh every now and then, my son. Don't forget that, either."

With that, he took off in a joyous, uncontrolled sprint. I will never forget his raucous laughter as he accelerated wildly through the hairpin turns. Perhaps he felt his responsibility temporarily discharged—he had, after all, got me thinking, and I suspect that that was his main objective, and now he felt free to celebrate and revel in the afternoon sun. I attempted to catch Father Ralph to say thanks, but he gradually pulled away, intent only in negotiating the next turn. A few miles before Honaker, he gave me a wave, and turned down a narrow, partially shaded road. I stopped at the intersection and watched, as my Soul disappeared into the Appalachian wilderness.

Rosedale, Virginia

When a friend calls to me from the road
And slows his horse to a walk
I don't stand still and look around
On all the hills I haven't hoed,
And shout from where I am, "What is it?"
No, not as there is time to talk.
I thrust my hoe in the mellow ground,
Blade-end up and five feet tall,
And plod; I go up to the stone wall
For a friendly visit.

—Robert Frost,
A Time To Talk

"How much further?" I screamed at Dave.

It was Saturday night on the road to Rosedale, Virginia. Dave and I had planned to end the day in Honaker, but the lack of accommodations forced us on to Rosedale, ten miles further down the road. In Honaker, we had noticed a group of local beer drinkers and stopped to ask for directions.

"Mowtel? Naw, thar ain't been no mowtel in Hownaker in four er five yeers. Thar wuz a bordin room downtown, tho. Didn' Miz Fannie Mae sell thet thang?" He had asked us the question as if we knew Fannie Mae intimately.

We thanked them for their help, pedaled a few blocks, checked the map, and continued on to Rosedale.

Jacked up, souped up, mufferless cars roared by us at alarming speeds. I checked my map again to make sure we weren't back in Indianapolis. Occasionally, a derisive yell came from one of the adolescent drivers. Dave and I have been on better highways during our trip. It was a relief when we collapsed on the steps of The Oaks motel office.

"Well, how ya'll doing?". Sorry to keep ya waitin'. My folks are at a family reunion and they left me in charge. They should be back shortly. Whatchya'll need?"

An attractive, forty year old woman delivered the message in one breath. How did she say all of that without breathing, I wondered.

"We'd like a room for the night please, ma'am." I handed her my credit card—it was my turn to pay.

"Well, of course, we gotta room for ya! Aw shoot! A credit card? I'm not sure I kin operate that blasted machine! My momma usually handles that, and she's not gonna be back till later. She's at the family reunion."

Barbara was a whirling dervish. In the time she spent telling us of her problems with the credit card machine, she had gotten it out, run the card, and handed it back to me. She also gave us a room key.

"Now 'bout the key. The lock on the door doesn't work, but everything will be awright. If ya'll want some supper, we stop serving early on Saturday, so hurry up."

"What time do you stop serving?" I asked, not wanting to miss a meal.

"Oh, it varies hon, we'll stay open for you, but hurry." she replied.

Dave and I hustled to the room with the broken lock. It is shocking pink on the inside. I note this for historical reasons only. We are not choosy and pink is most acceptable to us. We cleaned up and walked across the parking lot to the restaurant.

"I see ya'll made it. What kin I getcha to drink?" the amazing Barbara inquired. In addition to the motel job, she was also our waitress for the night. She hadn't slowed down, though. Before we could say "iced tea," the glasses were in front of us, along with the one-page menus.

Dave and I were not impressed with the choices. The most appealing item on the menu was ribeye steak, but the side dishes were all fried. We explained to Barbara our aversion to fried food.

"Well ya'll are in luck. Momma just walked in, and I'll send her over."

Her mother, Betty Brown, in addition to managing the motel, was also the cook at the restaurant.

"Hi fellas. What can I do for you."

She was soft spoken, with pretty features and a warm smile. In short, the type of person that makes you feel right at home. We explained about trying to avoid fried food during our trip.

Betty said, "Well, I think we might have some string beans left over from the family reunion, would ya'll like some of those?"

We began to feel better. Smiling, we nodded emphatically.

Feeling encouraged, she continued, "How 'bout some baked beans and potato salad, I might even have some more macaroni salad?"

"Yes! Yes!" we cried. None of these items were on the menu.

For the price of steak and fries, we were served ribeye steak, baked beans, string beans, potato salad, macaroni salad, and the best apple cobbler with ice cream I have ever tasted. We were grateful because she didn't have to go to the trouble of preparing all of this for us. Particularly after a long day at a family reunion.

Barbara told her father, Carson, about our trip, "Can you believe it? Ridin' bicycles across the country? Are they stupid, or whut?"

Carson inquired, "How did ya'll like Big A Mountain?"

"Not much," I replied. Then I told her why.

Despite our extreme physical fatigue, Dave and I, for what seemed to be the hundredth time, started to climb yet another hill. Only this one was different. This was a monster. Steep stacked switchbacks coiled on top of each other in a spiraling ascent to the sky. Riding next to each other, we said little. Only an occasional "damn" or "hell" was exchanged. Wiping sweat was a waste of time.

"Ya'll ere crazy!" Close to the top, an attractive young girl in her late teens leaned out of a car window and laughed at us. That was a first for the trip, and neither of us had the energy to reply. The terrain did change dramatically, however, when we crested "Big A" mountain. The land began to look more like open farmland, and less like the dark shadows of moonshine country.

We shared some of our favorite stories with the few customers that were in the restaurant. From time to time, Barbara or Betty refilled our iced tea and stopped to listen, or perhaps to ask a question or two.

"How 'bout some more o' that apple cobbler?" she said, "You know, I just finished making banana puddin' for tomorrow, would y'all like some of that, too?"

I thought we'd died and gone to heaven. Dave and I could barely move. We told her no, thank you. What an unexpected pleasure! After paying the bill—twenty dollars for us both—and leaving a generous tip, we waddled back to the pink room with no lock and slept soundly.

The next morning, we returned to the restaurant for breakfast. Carson was drinking coffee and reading the Sunday paper. We ordered pancakes, eggs, homemade biscuits with "sawdust gravy," and orange juice. It was one of the best morning meals of our trip. Our large glasses of orange juice were refilled at no additional charge.

As we dawdled over our last cup of coffee, Dave and I talked about how small kindnesses make all the difference. We also knew that this was the best and possibly our last "mom and pop" motel, and we were reluctant to leave it behind. We suspect that we are in for another day of cold and indifferent encounters with the inhabitants of Appalachia.

We left Barbara, Betty and Carson Brown, the hospitality of Rosedale, Virginia and pedaled away into the misty, warm Appalachian morning.

The Country Store

In my mind I'm going to Carolina,
Can't you see the sunshine,
Can't you just feel the moonshine,
Ain't it just like a friend of mine,
To hit me from behind,
Yes, I'm going to Carolina in my mind.

—James Taylor
Carolina In My Mind

Despite being only fifteen miles from Oxford, North Carolina, I had to get out of the heat. My body had sprung the last leak, and the two hundred ounces of liquid I had earlier consumed was history. Even the water I carried offered no relief. In the scorching Carolina sun, plastic water bottles heat, causing a gulp of water to taste like warm radiator fluid.

Dave agreed, and we pulled into The Country Store.

There wasn't much to the store. The three aisles were sparsely stocked with canned goods, bread, and other essentials. Off to the right, arranged in a circular fashion, were several straight backed chairs with slat seats. Missing was the card table—the setup begged for a game of checkers or gin. Perhaps in the morning the chairs are filled with tobacco farmers. Like their counterparts out west, they all talk about the weather or who got the most rain. In the winter, it is a good bet there are heated discussions about the outcome of the next basketball game between Duke and North Carolina State.

We eased into a couple of chairs, joining a small boy—perhaps eleven or twelve years old—and his grandfather. They informed us that we were the first cross country cyclists they have met. The boy was quiet and respectful, but showed a keen interest in our trip. He reminded us of the Popsicle Gang in Illinois. They, too, were polite and well mannered. From time to time, the grandfather asked a few of the standard questions. He would give proper consideration to our answers, and then turn to his grandson and ask for his opinion.

"Wouldn't you like to go on a trip like that?" he asked the small boy.

His grandson sunk down a few inches in the chair and shook his head. "Nooo!"

I don't know why, but the young boy made me think back to when I was his age. We were living in Raleigh then, not more than a hundred miles from the Country Store. I had three best friends back then, and we were always planning great adventures. If someone had asked us about going cross country on a bike, we all would have stuffed a sandwich in our handlebar bag and taken off. Rob would have gone the furthest because he had a three speed. Ed, Jeff and I wouldn't have made it out of the subdivision.

Other locals drifted into the Country Store. Many came by and said hello, and others waved or nodded. Several were absolutely incredulous over our adventure. The scene reminded me of Dave's Corridor Theory and again made me think back to my youth.

In 1967, I was just old enough to play Little League baseball. We had three blacks on our team—Handy, Preston, and Bernard. They were all great baseball players, and were good fellows on top of that. Being kids, we didn't think anything of the situation. It wasn't until years later that I realized 1967 was a period of racial unrest with marches, sit-ins, and demonstrations. Every time I take out my old pictures, I wonder about those three guys. What corridors had they selected?

By the time we finished our last fig newton, there were perhaps fifteen people in the Country Store. Dave and I felt refreshed and ready to go after our forty-five minute break.

As we were getting on our bikes, a big black guy drove up, got out of his car and asked, "How fer y'all bin ridin'?"

"Thirty-five hundred miles, so far," I said, "and we're not finished yet. We're headed to New Bern to finish our cross country ride."

"Naw, I can't believe it!"

He walked in the store and about fifteen seconds later, the big white guy who a few minutes earlier had ignored us, ran out yelling, "How fer did y'all say y'all'd come?" We gave him the short story and pedaled away into the hundred plus mid-afternoon heat. I turned around to get one last look at The Country Store. I was glad I did. The large glass window was lined with our curious friends. All four of them, the grandfather and grandson, the big black guy and the big white guy stood inside the store gazing out with looks of disbelief as we pedaled away. I gave our wide-eyed friends one last wave before we pedaled down the shimmering highway.

191

Roommates Relax

This land is your land, this land is my land,
From California, to the New York island,
From the redwood forest, to the Gulf Stream waters;
This land was made for you and me.

—Woody Guthrie,
This Land is Your Land

I don't remember the exact location where Dave and I realized that we were going to complete our journey. I recall we were both ecstatic when we crossed into Virginia. Perhaps that was due to the relief of being out of Kentucky.

It is not easy cycling in North Carolina. The heat and humidity make pedaling in the afternoon a real effort. The roads are a bit more congested and narrower than we like. Then too, this is all familiar territory for me. I am ready for the trip to be over.

Our last full afternoon on bicycles we spent pedaling past tobacco farms on our way to Greenville, North Carolina. They are like poor cousins of the rich, opulent farms that we passed out west.

In the afternoon, another friendly person reminded us of all the little encounters that have made our trip so special. We were on a county road, not far from Greenville, when a black man in his thirties came out of nowhere to take our picture. In an effort to give him a good shot, I knocked the air pump off my frame. It gave us a good reason to stop and talk.

Taking pictures just happens to be his hobby. Never had seen cyclists outfitted like us before, he explained, so he felt we were worth a shot or two. He was excited when we told him what we had done, and how close we were to finishing.

"Aw man," he said, "Y'all 'ave almost made it!" He wanted to know about the trip, what we were carrying in our panniers, and all the other questions that we have answered many times before. We chatted for a few minutes, and then continued our trip. Damn, this is an impressive accomplishment!

Around 6:00 p.m., we pulled into Greenville. It is a large town by our standards, offering a wide selection of hotels. The thought of camping never entered our minds. We settled on the Holiday Inn. I walked up to the desk with the sound of victory in my voice and shouted at the clerk, "We've just ridden our bicycles across the United States! We're tired and worn out, and we want the best rate you've got!"

The manager, who walked in just in time to hear me, said, "$29.95."

Together, we shouted, "We'll take it!"

It was the nicest motel of the trip. It came with a swimming pool, jacuzzi, and a nice restaurant. The regular rate was $56. Dave and I wheeled into our room, put our feet up, popped open the first two beers from an icy six pack, and celebrated our last hundred mile day of cycling.

We were two happy bikers. What could we possibly say after all we had done? We slowly sipped our beers, and reminisced about the special people and places that we have experienced.

We laughed about our old friend Jay. We could still hear his incredulous voice saying "Waddya mean you're not on a budget!" If he could only see us soaking in the luxury of a Holiday Inn. He would've had us sleeping on the grass. That was a sobering thought.

Or the honeymooners. Dave and I got out our maps, and figured that they were probably in North Dakota by now. We have a great deal of respect and admiration for their determination. I said a silent prayer on their behalf.

What else could we say about Liz Parenteau, or Dave Lorenz? Or the lady at the Parshall Motor Inn in North Dakota? These people, with their open kindness, provide the film footage of our memories. Conversations with them, the hellos and the good–byes, and all in–between, are cherished memories. Either we have been incredibly fortunate on our trip, or there are many special people in this country. I suspect that it is the latter.

But many other people have also made our trip special. We each remember strangers met along the way that for some reason, made an impression. If Liz, Dave and the others we met provide the film footage, then these friendly strangers are the sound track of our journey.

One such person was the motel manager who immediately tossed me the keys to her truck when she learned that Dave had bike trouble a few miles up the road. "Thought it might help out," she said.

Dave was impressed when I drove up next to him to see if he needed a lift.

Or the restaurant owner in Lansing, Iowa, that had a waitress deliver pizza to our motel room so we wouldn't have to pedal in the dark. The owner swore us to secrecy, "We don't normally deliver pizza." We sat on the back porch of the Shady Inn motel and enjoyed our meal.

Of the thousands of people that passed us on the highway, many waved, honked and virtually all gave us a wide berth. Even in my least favorite state, Kentucky, the drivers were exceptionally courteous.

Truck drivers deserve special thanks. Many times we heard the drivers behind us, gearing down their vehicles, waiting for just the right time to pass. We never had one truck honk at us during our trip, and none came close to running us off the road.

We talked, too, about the many places we passed along the way. The rich fertile lands of Washington State, the splendid beauty of Glacier National Park, the haunting beauty of the plains, the wandering Mississippi, the bountiful farmlands of Illinois and Indiana, the stark reality of Appalachian poverty, and the flat coastal plains of North Carolina. These places provide the mosaic upon which to place our snapshots and footage.

It has been quite a trip. We sipped on our last beer with just a little sadness. The next day would bring great joy, but it would also mark the end of a lifelong dream. Talk died out, with private memories occupying our thoughts. We each took our last swallow of beer and headed out the door to get some dinner. With a sad smile, I closed the door to the room and our last full day.

We've Never Been Bashful

"It's a poor dog that can't wag its own tail."

—Bill Fitzpatrick
—Dave Fooshe

We were only thirty–five miles from the end point of our journey. My parents, mother–in–law, Leith and Molly, and a newspaper photographer were planning on us being in New Bern at noon. Dave and I looked forward to a nice, easy day.

Yup. It was a good plan.

Our first mistake was thinking we would knock out our television interview in just a few minutes. Never the modest ones, my parents had arranged for a local New Bern television station to do a feature on us as part of their 4th of July newscast. The film crew met us on a county road in North Carolina. Actually, it wasn't really a film crew. It was one guy that alternately would drive and then take the video. We never stopped or talked—he just motioned for us to continue cycling. After shooting a scene, he would jump in the truck, race ahead of us, and shoot some more. It got to be a lot of fun.

It got to be too much fun. Dave and I were too busy waving at the cameras, feeling like the big shots, to notice that we were not heading towards New Bern. When we finally stopped to talk to Paul, the photo journalist, we realized we had missed a turn and had no idea where we were. As it turned out, neither did he.

For the next hour or so, though, we did the interview segment of the story. We really enjoyed this part. We took turns with the microphone, and answered the many questions that Paul asked. It didn't take him long to get us started. He might mention a word such as "weather," and Dave or I would launch into a spontaneous fifteen minute talk about the thunderstorms in Minnesota. Each of us had a lot of extra words stored up after our long, sometimes lonely trip.

By the time we finished with Paul it was 11:30 a.m. We still didn't panic, though, because we figured, at most, we were only fifteen miles away. That would put us in New Bern about 12:30. We pedaled off in what we thought was the general direction of New Bern.

By noon, we determined we were lost. Oh, Zeus, why us? Why now? Hadn't we paid our dues? When we finally found our way, we averaged twenty-one m.p.h., and arrived in New Bern at 1:15 p.m., over an hour late. It was not the kind of finish that Dave and I had envisioned. No, we wanted to finish ten to fifteen minutes early, with barely a bead of sweat dampening our shirts. Instead, we finished with soaked T–shirts, heaving chests, and beet red faces. We had an escort for the last mile of the trip. My dad had become frantic, and had driven out to look for us. He followed us the last mile and on to the finish line.

We made it! We turned the corner, and saw the waiting crowd. Only the newspaper photographer looked miffed at our late arrival. Molly was waving the American flag and running around in circles. Leith was beaming from ear to ear—she was so proud of me. And my parents? Well, I think they were just pleased to see me in one piece.

Dave and I spent two days in New Bern. It felt great, lying around, eating a lot, and telling all, "how we did it." It was a heady period. We talked to newspaper reporters, watched ourselves on television, and enjoyed being the center of everyone's attention. We savored our celebrity status.

And why not? We earned it. We deserved our day in the sun.

Epilogue

In some respects, writing about this trip has been even more satisfying than the actual journey. On many occasions, I worked past midnight, the time passing as quickly and easily as a cyclist sailing along with a steady tailwind. On one of these late night occasions, I closed my eyes, pushed away the keyboard, and thought some more about the trip.

If someone asked me about the highlights of my life, I could quickly come up with three or four significant events that are not only highlights, but also say something about the person that I am. I suspect this is true for most people, we all have defining experiences. Whether accomplishments or failures, they summarize the individual days of joy and sorrow. So it is with our adventure. Three years after our journey, a few special people and places come to mind.

*   *   *

One such place was Towner, North Dakota. It has come to represent all of the small, struggling towns we passed along U.S. Highway 2. This was the town that couldn't find a pharmacist to replace the one that had left. After considering this matter for the better part of a year, I decided I had to know. One afternoon, I called the Towner police station.

"Hi, I'm a few miles down the road, and I'm headed your way. I need to get a prescription filled, do you have a drugstore in town?"

"Sorry," the woman said. "We do have a drugstore, but our pharmacist left over two years ago and we haven't been able to find another one. You might check in Rugby. I think they'll be able to help you."

*   *   *

The honeymooners.

I will never forget this group. No one was going to tell them what they couldn't do, or that they didn't have the skills to cycle across the country. No one was going to tell the girls to lose a few pounds, and then think about the trip.

Their struggles actually went beyond those described in this book. After the trip, we learned that Ricky had also encountered the honeymooners. Our young friend was not with us when Dave and I had initially met the group.

"I was near Libby, Montana," Ricky said, "when I saw some cyclists behind me. My leg was really hurting, so I was only pedaling with one leg. Many times I'd even walk my bike up a hill, and then coast down the other side. I didn't stop to wait for the group. Every time I stopped to rest, my knee would tighten up. Can you believe it? Even though I was only using one leg, it took the honeymooners a whole day to catch up with me."

"Gosh, we're glad to finally meet you," they said. "We've been following you for a couple of days now, and have really been pushing ourselves to catch you."

Our young friend stayed in touch with the honeymooners. They did indeed finish the trip. On August 22, a full six weeks after Dave and I finished our journey, they happily pulled into Jamestown, Virginia, with their mission accomplished.

Salutes!

*   *   *

And our young friend Ricky?

He spent a couple more days in Glacier National Park, before catching a train back to Seattle, and then flying home. While in Glacier, he did what he enjoys most—camping and hiking. For historical purposes, it is important to note that his hair–raising experiences did not stop when he arrived in Glacier. True to form, he got lost while hiking on a remote, unmarked trail, in grizzly bear country. He took a spectacular photo of a never–before–seen–by–civilization glacier. The only bad news was that after taking the photo, he lost his balance, and camera, as he slid two hundred yards down the face of the glacier.

"It was a fun ride," he told us later.

Dave and I were, once again, shaking our heads.

"Never did find the camera," he explained. "And it took me almost the entire day to climb back up to the trail. I didn't realize how lost I was until I was talking to a ranger when I got back. He informed me that the area was closed to the public because of grizzly attacks and that no one had been back in that area in thirty years. It worked out OK, though.

"I have no regrets about not finishing the trip," Ricky says today. "I know you guys were intent on going from coast to coast, but I was happy just to be along for the adventure. Someday I will do what you've done. But, right now, I get a great deal of satisfaction in knowing what I've accomplished."

Ricky is now a graduate student at University of California at Berkeley. He is on a full scholarship majoring in Environmental Engineering.

*   *   *

I called directory assistance in Pontiac, Illinois. This will be easy, I thought. I'll just call the operator, get the phone number for the Meister family, and mail them the approval form for including their chapter, *The Popsicle Gang*, in the book. I was sipping on a cup of coffee when the operator answered.

"Can I help you?" she asked.

"Absolutely," I said. "Could you please give me the number for the Meister family near Pontiac?"

"There are three Meisters in Pontiac, which one would you like?"

"Give me all the numbers," I said. I didn't have any idea what I was getting into. I took another sip of coffee, and confidently dialed the first number.

"Hello," the first Meister said.

"Hello," I responded. I explained that I was writing about the Meister family that lives on a quiet country road near Pontiac. "Their boys," I said, "pass out free Popsicles to passing cyclists. I thought it would make a good chapter in the book. Is this the right number?" I clicked off the boy's names.

"Er, I don't know those boys," Mr. Meister said.

I took a full hit of coffee. "Well, are there any other Meisters in the area?"

"Yes there are, but you really need to talk to Rose, she can explain. Let me give you her number," he said, helpfully, and hung up.

I placed the phone down. What's going on here? I checked my map again. Pontiac is the only city anywhere near the county road where Dave and I met the boys. How many Meisters could there possibly be? I shook my head, took a final swallow of coffee, and dialed the number for Rose.

"Hello?" a woman answered. It sounded like an elderly lady. She confirmed that she was Rose Meister. I explained why I was calling.

"Give me those boy's names again?" she said. I did. "I don't know what to tell you—I don't know them."

"Tell you what," I said, "could you just give me the names of all the Meisters that live in the area?"

"I can't do that," she said. "It would take too long, and besides, I don't know them all anyway."

"How many are there?" I asked.

"Oh, there must be hundreds," she laughed, and then proceeded to give me a complete history of the Meister clan. During her briefing, I pushed the button on my phone that says "Speaker," walked into the kitchen, and made a fresh pot of coffee. I briefly stared at the liquor cabinet, returned to my desk, and dutifully listened to the last ten minutes of Meister history. I was halfway through my second cup from the fresh pot when she finished.

"Phew," I said, "could you give me your best guess of which Meister I should call?" She furnished me with a couple of possibilities. I thanked her for her time, and we hung up.

Several hours later, I finally reached the right Meister family. It was Ernie that answered the phone. I explained that I wanted their approval to include their chapter in the book.

"I'll talk to Mom, and I'll be right back!" he said.

A few minutes went by. I could hear some discussion in the background, but couldn't understand what was being said. Ernie came back.

"She said it's OK," he said. "Is there anything else you need?"

I looked again at my release form. It just isn't worth the trouble, I thought. I thanked him and hung up. I immediately called Dave and told him the complete story of the Meisters. By this time I was shaking, from caffeine and exasperation. I was looking for a consoling comment or two, but instead, Dave let me have it.

"Did you get all their addresses?" he asked. I told him no.

"Well you should have, you idiot. Think of all the books we could have sold. A book to every Meister in Illinois would represent enough to get us on the New York Times best seller list. I don't know how you make a living in sales."

I hung up, and swore I'd never again stop to talk to a small boy offering a free Popsicle.

*   *   *

Finally, there is Liz Parenteau.

Dave and I will never forget this kind woman from Harlem, Montana. If Towner represents the small, struggling towns, the honeymooners represent American optimism, and Ricky and the Popsicle Gang, the enthusiasm of youth, then what does Liz represent?

Perhaps it is the virtue of Hope. She had, after all, returned to her hometown, because she thought she could make a difference.

It could also be that she represents the virtue of Charity. She took two strangers into her home, and gave of what she had. Many people wouldn't have done what she did. It is always easier to say "No," and go on about your business, than it is to say "Yes," and expose yourself to a measure of risk. Dave and I will never forget Liz's expression when we treated her to breakfast in town. Her pride was evident—she had shown the skeptics that it is possible to be kind to strangers.

I called the operator and asked for her number.

"I'm sorry, sir," she said, "but we don't have a Liz Parenteau in the directory."

How could that be, I wondered. It is not likely that she moved. I called the police station.

"Ma'am, I'm trying to get in touch with Liz Parenteau," I said, "could you help me?"

There was a long pause. "I'm very sorry, but she passed away about six months ago. It was rather sudden. She got sick, and then died soon after."

I didn't know what to say, so I mumbled something about how I came to meet her, and what she had done for two tired cyclists.

"She was something special," the woman said. "She was always helping strangers, and other people in need. A town like ours does not replace a Liz Parenteau easily, if at all. She is missed." We talked a few more minutes, and then said good-bye.

I called up Dave and gave him the news. He was stunned.

"She was really a nice lady," he said, "and you like to think that people like her will always be there should you decide to go back for a visit. She not only believed she could make a difference in her town and in peoples' lives, but she had wanted to run for Mayor. We need more people like her in this country."

Dave is right, we need more people like Liz Parenteau.

*   *   *

"That's it," I exclaimed to Dave. "The book is done!" I had just selected the last photograph. It was the one of Father Ralph. It was now time to take the book to the printers.

Dave leaned back in his chair, stared at a me for a brief moment, and slowly shook his head. I could tell something was bothering him. It looked like he had unfinished business with me, business that couldn't wait a day or two. Or to be more precise, couldn't wait until we got the final copy to the printers. In fairness, though, I knew the photograph of Father Ralph, and indeed, everything about Father Ralph irritated the heck out of Dave. Engineers are a lot different than salesmen. I am proud to be part of a profession that can take the truth to the limits, and when no one is looking, sneak over the line, if just for a second. Why, no long term harm is usually done! Not so with engineers. If they step over the line, bridges collapse, skyscrapers topple, and lawyers move in. I'm not sure which of the three possibilities is the worst, either. Anyway, for whatever reason, Dave had never been pleased with my stories about Father Ralph.

"Dave, is there something on your mind?" I asked in my most innocent, angelic voice.

"You know what it is. It's that last photo."

"Oooohhhhhhh. You mean the picture of Fath..."

"He never existed. You know it. Our readers know it. Yet, here is a photo of this person you call Father Ralph.

"Dave, there's the truth, and then there's the truth."

"I hate salesmen."

I got serious when he said that. "Does Father Ralph exist? He does for me, and I'm glad he does. He is there to prick my conscience, point out my hypocritical positions, and in short, be a guide in the search for my soul."

"Then you agree that this is a bogus picture. There is no Father Ralph, and we can save a few dollars by leaving out the photo."

"In an absolute sense, Dave, you are right. That picture really isn't Father Ralph, it's a picture of Dr. Al Masters, the minister at St. Andrews Presbyterian Church in Greenville. He just happens to be my current "Father Ralph." Anticipating his next question, I continued.

"I went to Catholic school for a number of years, Dave, and learned about Christianity from this upbringing. But the search for the soul is a human condition, one that certainly is bigger than a specific religion. I just enjoyed bringing a certain amount of the good old "Catholic angst" to the topic.

Dave sighed, and then nodded.

"All right, Father Ralph can stay."

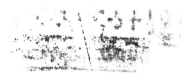